Ou Darkness

My Escape From Sin

This is my personal account of my life before giving myself to Jesus Christ.

Drugs, sex, and rock and roll were all I lived for until God opened my eyes.

From the streets as a panhandler, to touring America with The FROST, to joining Scientology in Detroit, Michigan as a staff member...

To the day Jesus Christ set me free!

JN.8:36
Therefore if the Son makes you free, you shall be free indeed.

Proverbs 14:12 (NKJV)

There is a way *that seems* right to a man,
But its end *is* the way of death.

All scriptures are taken from the NKJV, unless noted

1 PETER 2:9

BUT YOU ARE A CHOSEN GENERATION, A ROYAL PRIESTHOOD, A HOLY NATION, HIS OWN SPECIAL PEOPLE, THAT YOU MAY PROCLAIM THE PRAISES OF HIM WHO CALLED YOU OUT OF DARKNESS INTO HIS MARVELOUS LIGHT;...

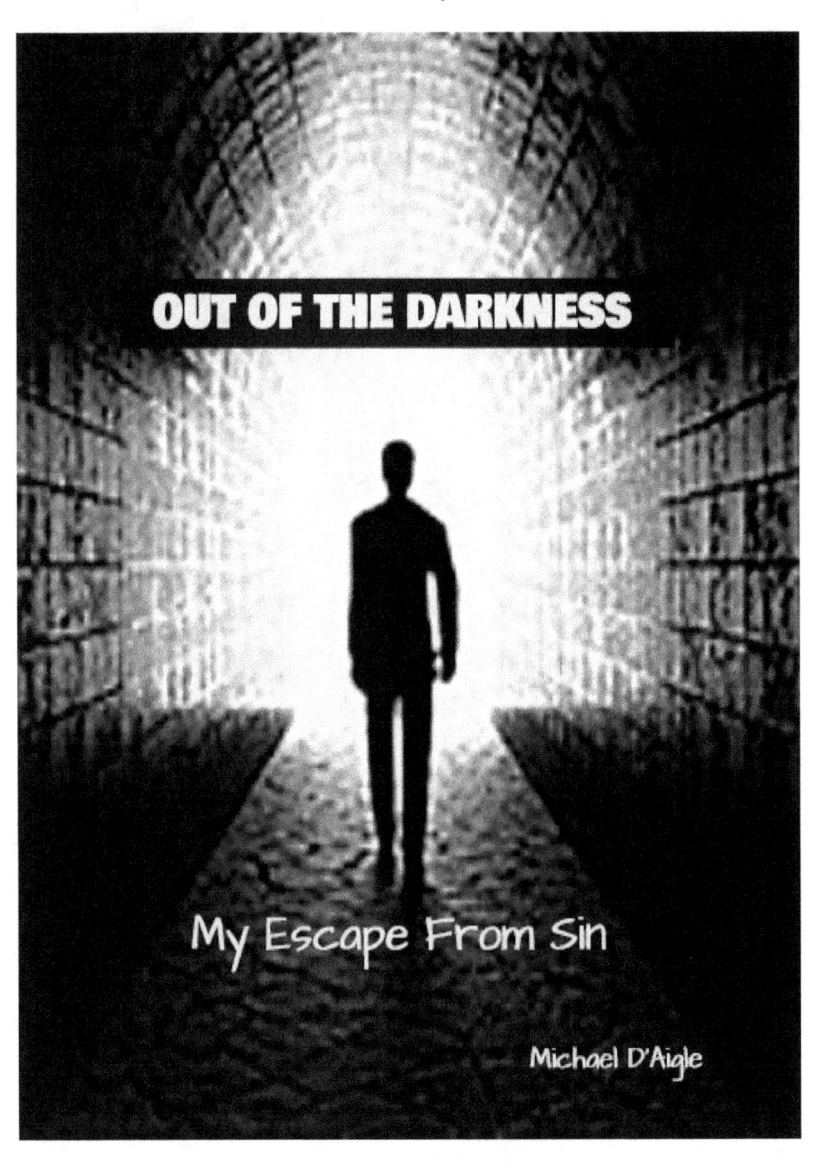

OUT OF THE DARKNESS

My Escape From Sin

Michael D'Aigle

WHY I WROTE THIS BOOK...

"Return to your own house, and tell what great things God has done for you." And he went his way and proclaimed throughout the whole city what great things Jesus had done for him. **Luke 8:39**

My reasons for writing this personal story of mine are motivated by the sincere belief that by sharing my own personal experiences with drugs, the secular world of rock, and my involvement with Scientology; I may be able to keep others from being snared and taken captive by sin. What may first appear to be beautiful and alluring – may end up being your worst nightmare... that was the case with me.

Deciding what to use as the title for this book "Out Of The Darkness" was very easy because that is exactly what God did. He rescued me from a world of fear, anxiety, and dread; that can only be fitly described as a cloud of darkness that I was living under before I surrendered my life to Jesus Christ.

The subtitle - "My Escape From Sin," was much more difficult to choose because there were many things that I needed to be set free from. Drugs, sexual sins, my worship of rock music, and my involvement in Scientology; were some of my biggest struggles, but in truth – there were many other things in my life that needed to change.

I didn't know it then, but my life was tangled up in so many ungodly ways; that I couldn't see that music had become the center of everything I did – from the time I opened my eyes in the morning – till the wee hours of the morning when I laid my dope filled eyes to sleep. Music – rock music in particular was an idol – a god that my life revolved around.

Last, but not least was my anger and bitterness towards my father for forcing me to leave home as a young man barely seventeen. I was a long way from forgiving him for that; and it would be a long and painful road to hoe before I dealt with that issue. Yes indeed, I needed to escape from many things, but it was my involvement with Scientology that left me feeling totally desperate and depressed about everything.

5

Much of this book deals with how I became entangled into the seductive web of Scientology; and how I managed to escape by the grace of God. Sadly, my cousin became heavily involved in Scientology and died before he could escape from the lethal grip it had on his life. I tried to warn him years ago about Scientology being a "cult" that he needed to get out of; but he like so many others – rejected my warnings to his own peril...

Some of the things I share in this book were not easy to share, and reveal events in my past that I'm ashamed of – things I did when I was lost, clueless – and speeding straight towards hell.

This book may not make you laugh, and it may make you wince or cringe at the depths of sin and depravity that I was trapped in; but it will open your eyes to the subtle and seductive appeal that Scientology, and all other false religions have...

I can tell you the reader this simple truth before you begin to read my story of how God delivered me out of a life of excess and lawlessness, and the cult of Scientology. that getting out of a religious cult or false religion is much, much harder than it is getting into one!

All of us know someone who is either involved with a religious cult of some kind, contemplating joining one; or is a member of any number of false religions that are not in agreement with the teachings of orthodox Christianity.[a] Hopefully this book may help someone you know avoid the horrors and damage that happens to a person who has unwittingly joined a religious cult.

Preventing someone from joining a cult, or false religion is easier than trying to rescue them once they're trapped into one. Sadly, leaving a cult or religious group that has taken you under their influence and control is very difficult to do!

---

a. **Orthodoxy**(from Greek ὀρθοδοξία, orthodoxia – "right opinion") is adherence to correct or accepted creeds, especially in religion. In the **Christian** sense the term means "conforming to the **Christian** faith as represented in the creeds of the early Church".

With that in mind, this book is meant to be shared, to expose the works of darkness, and to set the captives free! I ask you not to let it sit on a shelf, or in a drawer, but please pass it on to someone who may be struggling with drugs, alcohol, or anything that has them enslaved and in bondage.

I've tried to use scriptures to capture the essence of each chapter's main theme in this book; and there are some references both "footnotes & endnotes," to allow you to go deeper into an idea or particular thought that is being conveyed. These references can be found at the end of each chapter or at the end of the book.

My only regret in writing this book is that I didn't write it sooner, for that I'm truly sorry. My prayer for all who read this book is simple. I ask Almighty God to take use my testimony and the things I've experienced during my short time here on earth; to keep others from repeating the mistakes I made. May God expose the works of darkness, and the devices and schemes of Satan through the pages of this book.

At the end of this book are some fundamental elements of the Christian Faith that have been accepted as reliable sources by most Christians for centuries. The Apostle's Creed, The Nicene Creed, and many Christian classics are listed for anyone wishing to understand the Christian Faith better.

For Those Jesus Died For,

Michael D'Aigle

*Please note - Some of the names have been changed in this book, to protect their identities. An (*asterisk) will be found next to their name.

WHAT'S INSIDE...

CLUELESS

Every story has a beginning, and I would be amiss to not give you the reader a short glimpse of my life prior to my journey from Suburbia into the world of drugs, sex, secular rock and my involvement with Scientology. I won't go into all of the minute details of my childhood, but do think it's important to give a backdrop to the state of mind I was in during that period of my life.

I read somewhere, or perhaps it was in one of my college classes long after I had left Scientology; that most people go through life without really knowing what they want to do with their life. This large mass of humanity just ebbs forward, going from one event in their life to the next – without a clue. Millions of people living their entire lives without any real sense of purpose, or meaning; with "life happening to them" as they grow old.

That was me – that was our family.

Our family would be what most would consider middle class; with my father working as a fireman and my mother being a stay at home mother. In later years, she would go on to become a nurse; but during my parent's first years of marriage she was at home with us – myself and my three other siblings.

I'm the baby of the family, and I have two older sisters, and one older brother. I was a happy child and was blessed with a cheerful disposition; I really don't have many bad memories of my first few years here on earth... that was not the case for my older siblings as a traumatic and life changing event was soon to take place that would change all our lives forever.

My Mom Vanishes

At the age of three, I was motherless. I know that sounds a little bizarre; but in fact for a young lad of only three years of age – that is what it must have seemed like. One day my mother was holding me and laughing with me; and the next day I was living in a home with out my mom.

The truth is, I don't remember now her leaving, or being told that she had left... but I'm sure even in my little mind, I must have wondered where did my mommy go?

This simple, innocent understanding of what I was going through was not what my older brother and two sisters were experiencing because they were all much older than me. My brother was four years older, and my sisters were six and seven years older. It wasn't until years later that I found out where our mother had gone.

A Nervous Breakdown

I don't remember when I first learned where my mother had gone , the reasons for my mother's sudden departure from our lives – where she went – why she left us, and how our father handled that were revealed to me. For me, it didn't really seem very upsetting or disturbing; but it did raise a lot of questions that needed to be answered.

My innocence, being only three and my happy and cheerful disposition was a blessing to me during this time. These facts meant I was spared much of the emotional pain and heartache my three siblings all experienced because they were older.

I was later to discover that my poor mother suffered a complete mental and emotional breakdown. Her condition was so bad that my father under the advice of several psychiatrists, had her committed to a mental facility in Pontiac Michigan. My father with no real faith in God, and being convinced that our mother would never be sane or normal again; divorced my mother and went on with his life as best he could.

I was spared the terrible pain of missing my mother, only because I was too young to really have a deep bond with her. Sadly, my brother and sisters were affected by our mother's sickness and absence in ways that only they could explain to you. As I got older I could see the horrible effects that all of us had suffered by having our mother taken away from us when we all so young.

My father did his best to take care of all four of us, and made sure that all our basic needs were provided for. For that I'm grateful, he was a decent father in that regard. He never really talked much about God, religion, or faith; and the few times we went to church were not the norm – but rather the exception.

Sadly, for our family the Bible, prayer, and going to church were not something that my father encouraged us to do, and I now know that our family was "clueless" when it came to those kind of spiritual things.

I've often wondered what our family would be like today if my father had not divorced my mother? What if he had been a man of faith, a man who was not quick to listen to the voices of psychiatrists? What if he had prayed to God, and asked God to heal and restore my mother's mind.

I truly believe that had my father been a Christian who had a strong faith in God and His word – the Holy Bible; all of our lives would have taken a different path. I don't have any resentment or anger towards my now deceased father; as I'm sure under the circumstances he was doing the best he could with four children and a wife who for all practical purposes – was not here, not mentally or emotionally anyways.

Now looking back, as we all do at what might have been if only... I know that my father did not have a great spiritual foundation in his own life and family growing up. I've learned from my mother and other relatives that my father's life growing up was filled with many disappointments and there was little or no spiritual guidance in his life.

A Big Blur...

Much of my childhood is a big blur, with most of my childhood memories somehow lost in time; and that can only be described as a kind of hazy fog – with months and years of my life simply gone forever. I've never understood why it's that way, but there are certain events etched clearly in my memory (like getting caught stealing at the grocery store, or when I nearly drowned in a lake up North in Michigan).

I don't remember our family going to church together, at least not on any regular basis. The few times we did go were so infrequent that they quickly faded into oblivion as is the case with isolated events in our lives.

My brief encounters with church and Christianity weren't bad , just too few to have any lasting effect or influence on me as a child.

In our home, about the only time we mentioned God or did anything related to faith or religion with any regularity might be one of us saying grace at the dinner table. It went something like this, someone would say, "Who wants to say grace?" And one of us would say jokingly - "grace". We would laugh or chuckle and then begin to eat our supper.

Sadly, God – church, and the practice of any kind of religious observance was not something we thought much about – and certainly didn't practice as a family. At that time in my life I have to admit it wasn't important to me, it's hard to miss something that really wasn't there in the first place.

Hello Mother

When I was around eleven, after years of hearing stories from my family about my mom, and what she was like; I was told that she was coming home. Wow, that had me very excited! I was finally going to meet my mom face to face. Truthfully, I couldn't remember what she was like or what she looked like. I anxiously awaited the day when we would finally meet face to face...

Meeting my mother who I really couldn't remember, was an exciting event that has always stayed with me; and for me it was a very positive and pleasant experience. My mom had red hair, and looked very beautiful to me; I was very elated to finally get to meet my mom and I wasn't disappointed. It wasn't long after this reunion that things changed drastically in my life.

My mom regained custody of me, and I moved away from my brothers and sisters and dad; and began living with my mom in downtown Flint, in lower Michigan. This was going to be short lived, but in the beginning I really liked being with my mom. I was content and happy to finally get to know my mom after years of not having a relationship with her.

It was at this time of my life that I began playing the guitar, and took lessons for a short period; just long enough to figure out how to play almost anything I heard on the radio or T.V.

My very first band, Mike's Bandits formed around this time, and we would play anywhere we could, from living rooms/porches, and backyards – for anyone who would endure our rough edges as newbies in the music business.

We were a scraggly 3 piece band, with lots of energy and zeal, and plenty of "bad notes" to remind everyone (including ourselves) – this was our very first band. This was to be the beginning of a crazy and zany musical journey that I'm still on even at this time in my life; though now as a Christian musician it's not so crazy as it is a blessing!

Finally, I had found something that I was passionate about, something that gave my life real meaning – something I could chase. Man O man did I ever chase it – music became the center of my universe, and I could think of little else at that time of my life.

A Short Reunion

My reunion with my mom started out great; but sadly it wasn't going to last very long. In less than two years from the time I had moved in with my mother; I found myself once again experiencing the loss of my mother. Only this time, I was old enough to know what was going on – to know that my mother was going to be taken away from me once again. This period of my life were the best of times, and sadly the worst of times...

My mother enrolled me in a parochial school in downtown Flint, Saint Michael's High School, and I attended religious services every school day and on weekends as well. Only a year or so earlier I had taken catechism classes and had been searching for something that I thought I would find in church. I was very sincere at this point in my life, and while I wasn't really close to God, or sensing any real changes or anything – I did have a belief that God was real, and that Christianity was very real and powerful.

That was my freshman year in high school, and I was cruising along with things going very well for me. I had a paper route that was giving me a good supply of money for buying guitars and other things a twelve year old young man likes to spend his money on. I was doing well in school, and life was good – very good. That was all about to come to a screeching halt!

I don't remember how it all began, but I do remember watching my mother disintegrate and fall apart before my very eyes. My mother was a nurse and seemed very happy with her new career that she had embarked upon since she had been released from the mental hospital years earlier.

Everyone was proud of what my mother had been able to do with her life, and now it was all about to unravel before my eyes – and it was surely something I was not prepared to experience.

My mother would stare off without any expression on her face, and begin mumbling and talking to someone... at least I thought she was talking to someone. I would try to engage her in conversation, and she wouldn't even hear me, or acknowledge that I was speaking to her.

That was unsettling and very scary for me. I began to realize that something very terrible was happening to my mom, and it was like having a bad dream – only it was all too real – all too horribly real.

A Very, Very Bad Day!

I've had a few very bad days in my life, like the day I couldn't walk or move because my back was so out of line that I was literally paralyzed. I could only move myself by crawling painfully on the floor from one place to another place; and that with the most excruciating pain imaginable. Or the time when I was stuck walking in the desert with no water, and with no one to help me get out of the hot scorching desert heat that burnt me to a crisp; and left my lips swollen and cracked for weeks.

Those were bad days to be sure, but the day I watched my mother have another nervous break down was worse! It has to be one of the worst days of my life, and certainly one of hers as well. They say there are "bad days", and then there are really "BAD DAYS!"... they (whoever they are) were right.

My mother didn't sleep for at least two or three days, and she was crying and writing a long letter to the pope, and rambling on about things that I couldn't understand. I knew she was not in her right mind, but at the age of twelve, and with no real knowledge of mental illness, or what to do in circumstances like I was facing – I began to panic. It was clear to me that my mother was having a nervous breakdown and that I needed to do something – and do it very quickly.

I called my father and told whoever it was that answered the phone(I don't remember exactly who it was); that mom was acting crazy and someone needed to come and help her. The rest of the day is a blur now, but I knew my life was about to change again and little did I know how drastic that change would be. I wasn't ready for those changes – but had no choice...

That was an extremely horrible day for my mother, me, and our entire family. I'm sure it brought back horrible memories for my father and siblings. For me it was an event that would change me forever.

I had lost my mom when I was only three, and now at the age of twelve – he was taken away from me once again. Only this time – I was no longer innocent of what was going on, no longer able to escape the pain of having to lose your mother to something that no one understood or wanted to talk about...

My happy life living with my mom came to a freaky end; and in my heart I knew that I was in for a rocky ride. This chapter of my childhood is forever etched in my memory as one of the most horrible things I've ever experienced, and profoundly affected the way I would look at things from that day forward.

There was no one to talk to so I just buried my emotions deep down in the back of my mind – I was not going to share what happened to my mom with anyone, not at that time anyways. Now I had an idea of how my siblings must have felt when my mother was taken away from them years earlier; when I was too young to know what was going on. Now I knew.

The good news for me was I knew I was going to be okay, that somehow I would survive. Partly because of my youth and the positive disposition I had been born with; but mostly I believe because God was with me during those awful dark days when my mother was falling apart before my very eyes. God was with me even though I never really prayed much or sought God during that time. God is merciful, and shows us His kindness even when we are unaware of it – or clueless of that fact.

I should add one more thing about my mom's ongoing fight with mental illness. When all this happened, there was still a lot of shame and embarrassment associated with anyone suffering with mental illness; it was for many families – something you just didn't talk about.

That was in addition to all of the other emotional garbage I was dealing with that every teenager has to go through. This became our "family's secret."

My life somehow became very troublesome and complicated. I really didn't want to have to explain to anyone what I had just went through with my mom, and it became something that I hid deep on a shelf in the back of my mind. I pushed the whole traumatic episode I had just experienced deep – deep into a corner that I rarely mentioned to anyone.

I'm not sure what happened to my mom, because part of me didn't want to know – part of me was frightened by what I had just lived through with my mom. It was freaky, strange, and something that I was ill prepared to deal with at that age. It wasn't until many years later that I found out the painful details of my mother's mental breakdown while I was living with her.

I do know that none of us went to visit my mother (at least not regularly)to my knowledge, and it was also something that none of us really wanted to talk about, especially me. All I knew was – they took my mom away again.

My mother's mental illness became something to be avoided when we got together as a family – which was becoming less and less frequent as we got older.

Every family has problems, I knew that – but that fact gave me no comfort because telling friends your mom was "crazy" was not something I wanted to share with anyone – least of all my friends.

Now before you the reader think I'm being crass or cruel referring to my mother as being "crazy" - please keep in mind that I'm simply letting you know how a 12 year old teenager thinks. That is how I thought about the entire episode with my mom having a mental breakdown right before my very eyes.

Years later, when I was older, I had a lot more sympathy for my mother, and for anyone who has suffered a nervous breakdown, or severe depression. It's funny how time can change the way you look at things – that was the case with me.

So now I had my mom taken away from me twice and I was barely going on 13 at the time. This time was different from when I was just a wee lad of three.

This time when my mother was taken away from me – I felt a deep dark sense of loss – something my older siblings surely must have experienced when my mother was first taken away from all of us.

One thing was certain – I would never think about mental illness the way I did before I witnessed my mother have a complete nervous breakdown. For years I would keep that part of my childhood to myself. It wouldn't be until many years later that I would be comfortable talking about that time of my life with anyone.

A WILD CHILD

And do not be conformed to this world, but be transformed by the renewing of your mind, that you may prove what is that good and acceptable and perfect will of God. **Romans 12:2**

If you look at something long enough it will influence you, for good or for bad; it all depends on what you're looking at. It's the same with what you listen to. The old axiom: Garbage in/Garbage out – is true. I was being conformed to the world around me – a very attractive and alluring world without a clue of what was happening to me.

To be sure, I wasn't reading the Bible or anything spiritually edifying, and I wasn't listening to Christian music. My eyes and ears were immersed in whatever was popular on the radio, T.V., and in the magazines I read.

Not surprisingly, I spent the next few years of my life making a series of bad decisions; decisions that would ultimately end with me destitute and lost - a child of the night. I was being conformed to the secular world's way of thinking and living; without ever realizing I was going in the wrong direction – straight to hell!

The transition for me from living with my mother where I was very happy and contented; to having to adjust to moving in with my dad was extremely disturbing and upsetting. I was a very confused and unhappy teenager, and scared at the idea of starting over. Sometimes, things happen in our life that we have no control over – and this was one of those times.

I had just come from living in a relatively disciplined atmosphere where attending religious services nearly everyday and on weekends was the norm – to a whole new life of few restraints or boundaries. I was about to enter a completely new world where drugs, sex, and rock music would be my universe; my life was going to be patterned after what I heard and saw all around me at that time. My life was about to get really crazy.

My father had remarried, and I now found myself living in a very unstable home with a step mother that I didn't get along with, and four new siblings, (a step brother and three step sisters). The Brady Bunch we weren't – and unfortunately; I don't remember anyone going to church regularly or reading the Bible. One thing was for sure – I wasn't into God or Jesus.

This was a replay of my life at home before I went to live with my mother, only now I had a different family to live with. To add to this, our home was a small ranch style home; and with seven of us living in close quarters – it only made things seem more uncomfortable.

I wasn't happy any longer with this living arrangement, and my father didn't seem that happy about my having to come and live with him again either... my relatively stable and happy life as I knew it was over. I went from living a relatively quiet life with just my mom and me; to living with four new siblings that were total strangers to me and like me, set in their ways. (all of us were in our teens) Adjusting to this new family situation was not easy for me, and I'm sure my dad picked up on that.

I was an average student for most of my school years, though I could have excelled had I really wanted to. School was quite boring for me, and I never really fit in with the "good kids", I was too wild for that. I wasn't great in sports, but I was good at playing guitar and singing.

I knew my father wasn't really impressed with me at this time – me with my long hair and funny clothes, and loud rock music! He had a hard time relating to me I'm sure, and we had a very cool relationship. We really were like two ships passing in the night; rarely speaking to one another.

My one companion and source of comfort was my music, my guitars and my rock music; and my nonconformist friends who most mothers warned their daughters not to associate with – really. Ironically, I went from going to a parochial school with it's rigid religious structure and instruction – to a secular high school where my moral compass was about to go spinning out of control.

That transition for me proved to be more than I could really handle. My best friend before I moved back with my father was going to go into a seminary to become a priest – really. Now, I was hanging out with friends that couldn't care less about God or anything to do with Jesus, or religion for that matter!

Looking back it's clear to see that the friends I chose to hang out with had a big influence on the next chapter of my life. My friends weren't violent or terribly bad people; they were just like me – restless souls who were not following the "good kids", and mostly from homes with little or no religious upbringing. In other words, we were all just a wild group of guys and girls into partying, getting high, and living on the edge.

The few friends I did have weren't Christians, at least not at the time; and almost everyone I knew was from a broken or dysfunctional home. I had only one close friend who had both parents(who had never divorced)living at home; and I just did not know what a normal – happy family was like.

Well, that's not entirely true. My other "best friend" - Pat had a great home compared to everyone I knew. I remember thinking, it must be nice going home to a normal home where mom and dad were both home and everyone ate dinner together. That simple and idealistic concept of what a "normal" family is like – was enforced by my friendship with Pat.

Later on, as I got older I did find a few friends that had relatively normal home lives; but again God – or church, and the Bible were not evident or something I remember seeing in any of my friends homes.

That I gravitated to other teens from broken and dysfunctional homes was quite natural, because to me that was normal... that was my comfort zone.

I chose to hang out with the misfits, the wild kids as moms and dads would like to call us. We banded together and isolated ourselves from the "nice kids , jocks and braniacs" and all the other clicks that we didn't fit in to.

The common denominator we all had though was drugs, rock music, and the fact that most of us came from "broken homes" – that was something we all had in common. Oh – and did I mention long hair?

I began to play in bands, and go to rock concerts (usually high on something) to see the big bands at the time, Rod Stewart, Jeff Beck, The Yardbirds, Bob Seger, Ted Nugent, and many other big names that would be at the festivals and popular clubs and concert halls .

Getting high and going to concerts became the thing that dominated my life at that time – those two things were where my heart and affections were focused. This is also where most of my time and money were spent.

Drugs and music had become gods to me – I bowed down to them, if not with my knees – then certainly with my heart and emotions. Little did I know then – but music – especially hard rock music had become the most important thing in my life. I can honestly say I was addicted to it.

Oh I should also mention my bedroom, it was one big collage of colors and lights; with psychedelic posters and pictures completely covering every inch of the walls and ceiling. This was my world – my place to escape from the normal world which at that time I felt more and more uncomfortable with. Tune in, Turn on, and Drop out was the mantra I lived by at that time.

The atmosphere was like stepping into another world – a world of loud rock music, flashing lights, that would make my friends smile as they came through the door. It was just a crazy place to retreat from the normal world around me that I was slowly finding unattractive. I was turning awayfrom the straight life most kids were on, and going in the other direction.

My father did not know what was going on in my bedroom into the early morning hours, and my step-mother never bothered me either. If they had known what my friends and I were doing, they may have stepped in and kept me from going deeper and deeper into the world of drugs, rock music, and experimentation that my friends and I were immersed in.

Children need boundaries and standards to keep them in line; but looking back I understand now that my father was just not prepared for the challenge of keeping me away from the bad choices I was making as a wayward teen. I'm not blaming anyone – just making a point that in our home there was no spiritual guidance – none.

I wanted my father's attention – craved his involvement in my life; and that void in my life certainly played a part in the bad choices I made later.

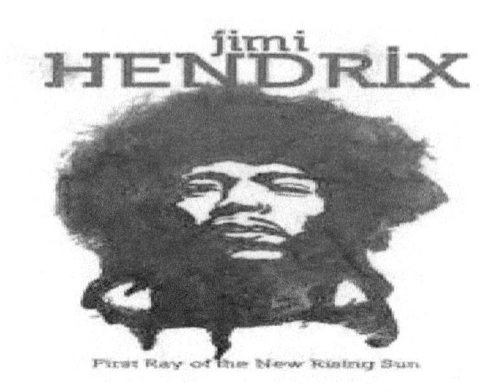

THE DARK SIDE OF ROCK MUSIC

When I was just fifteen I met Jimi Hendrix[1], who at the time was a rock guitar phenomenon – and touring with his band- The "Jimi Hendrix Experience." They were not your typical secular rock band, even at that time. Jimi Hendrix, was a black guitarist, and backed up by two white guys. Mitch Mitchell on drums, and Noel Redding on bass guitar. They released 3 albums, and turned the rock music on it's head with their "psychedelic" sound.

Many consider Jimi Hendrix to be one of the most creative and talented rock guitarist of all time; and some say he was in fact the best of the best! That may be true, but my first encounter seeing him in person in Flint, Michigan was a big let down to say the least. What was to be an exciting concert up close, with one of my favorite rock bands turned out to be my first look at what was really going on in the lives of many of my "heroes" within the secular rock world I worshiped...

That day is permanently etched in my memory forever. Jimi was apparently in a bad mood and was giving us(some of his fans) the middle finger from a window where his dressing room was; for reasons unknown? A handful of fans, including myself had shown up early to catch a glimpse of Jimi and the band before the concert, in the hope we might get to meet him, or get his autograph. To say we were shocked – would be an understatement...

I can't remember what I was thinking at the time, but I do remember us shouting for Jimi and the band to come to the window so we could wave at them and say hello.

To my surprise, Jimi did appear at the window in back of the auditorium where he was staying; which was probably his dressing room and suddenly appeared at the window from above. We were all shocked at what happened in the next few minutes; and it was one of those moment's in time; that I'll never forget!

There was Jimi Hendrix, standing – and giving all of us the middle finger. He was saying something, but we couldn't hear what he was saying from down below where we were standing. I was angry and disappointed to see someone I idolized and admired being so hostile and nasty towards his fans... Truthfully, it blew my fifteen year old mind.

Seeing my idol giving us the "middle finger" simply because we wanted to see him, should have opened my eyes to the kind of world I was enamored with – but at that time it didn't... it would take many years for me to realize the dark, devilish side of the secular rock industry. I was young and dumb and naive.

He only played four songs that day at this concert, and then only after making all of us in the audience wait for at least an hour, again for reasons unknown? He was having a bad day his manager said, but more than likely was stoned and not in his right mind. In any event, his behavior that day was what most of us in the rock world came to expect as "normal"...

I was used to being "freaked out" and having my mind blown away by weird and bizarre behavior and antics; which were part and parcel to the drug scene of that day. But, having Jimi Hendrix give me and other fans of his the middle finger was over the top, and really shook me to my core. I just pushed it to the back of my mind and didn't think about it much until years later.

My experience that day, of seeing my idol Jimi Hendrix act so twisted and mean towards us, his fans; should have sent "red flags" of warning all over the place! It didn't. When the concert was over, I waited for Jimi to come out and when he finally did; I ran over and shook his hand and gave him a slew of compliments about how much I liked his music.

My love for music blinded me!

If I had really had my head on straight, I would have left when I first realized that Jimi Hendrix was not a good role model to follow or look up to. Being young and dumb, and star struck – I just wrote it off as the way things were with rock musicians – with the rock -and-roll world I had fallen in love with. This was just a prelude to the dark side of the music that had me in it's spell.

I came to accept the idea that the rock music world was just that way. Vulgar, crude, and not very nice. I could say it more forcefully, but you get my point. In fairness, not every artist or band fit that negative stereotype – but sadly a large number of them did.

I would learn later first hand just how ungodly and unholy life could be living in the thick of the rock and roll world among the biggest stars at that time. Like the unsuspecting mouse going into a trap that has no way out – I was headed towards a world that was enticing and promising. It almost killed me and robbed me of everything I possessed.

Slowly but surely, I was drifting further and further away from whatever relationship I had once had with God, the Bible, and Christianity. I had once said I would never smoke cigarettes, and here I was not only smoking them, but doing other drugs and drinking alcohol as often as I could. I was living life in the fast lane, and I was not happy on the inside.

Okay, to be totally honest I was having fun living on the edge – pushing the envelope further and further with my like minded friends. But, deep inside there was no real peace or contentment; in reality I was a lost young man emotionally and spiritually. I found I could forget about that emptiness inside if I just kept doing things that the "good kids" weren't doing.

Not content just to be another rebellious teenager, I went out of my way to "freak people out." I remember walking down the hallway in school with a pair of dark sunglasses, dressed like I was in a prison uniform, and watching all the "nice kids" move over to the other side of the hall to avoid me. Shocking people was a big game that my friends and I played daily.

I was in fact, the kind of boy – young man, that mother's told their daughters not to hang out with. That was me, I couldn't agree more! Now, it's hard for me to admit to being a criminal; because at the time I didn't think of myself as being a bad person.

The problem was I was comparing myself to my friends, who were all doing the same things. I wasn't violent or into fighting, but stealing clothes and records; that was something I became very good at.

I was shoplifting at this time and staying out late at night with my friends till the wee hours of the morning. I would come home and retreat to my bedroom in the basement where I would listen for hours to my favorite bands. Most of my waking hours revolved around my world of music, girls, and drugs, and finding a new "high" was at the top of my list.

That I never was convicted of shoplifting is nothing short of amazing. Why? Because what had begun as just stealing a few records every now and then, had become a weekly obsession. My friends and I would go into stores downtown where we lived, and walk out with 10 to 20 albums. With every successful mission without getting caught – we would become more and more brazen and outrageous. I was proud of our slick and clever thievery, and we just kept stealing from more and more stores and the thrill of getting away with our thefts was addicting – it was some kind of high to us.

To be honest, the only reason I can remember for quitting our thievery was the simple fact we had stole almost every possible record we wanted... My record collection was a mile high! Well, not really but it was a massive stack of records that if I had been caught – surely would have put me in jail or prison for a long time. We were without shame, which today I find scary.

The bible talks about the "sins of our youth"; and man O man did I ever confirm the truth of that scripture in my life as a troublesome teen. It may have been better if I had been caught stealing, that may have been the dose of reality and discipline I needed; but that was not to be. It was simply one more crazy episode in my teenage years... I'm sure some of you reading this now can relate. PS.25:7

I'm sure my father had a hard time trying to deal with me at that time, but as strange as it may sound – I was hoping he would say something to me – anything. I was desperate to have a normal relationship with my father (whatever that was I wasn't sure). Unfortunately, my father and I hardly said a word to each other. That void in my life was definitely one reason why I was living such a rebellious and lawless lifestyle.

STONED OUT !

Along with our zany clothes and hair, my friends and I were very keen on experimenting and trying the latest thing: Getting stoned! We starting using marijuana on a regular basis, and then went on to use psychedelic drugs like LSD, and peyote, mescaline, and other hallucinogenic drugs whenever we could afford them. Life was getting more complicated, and maintaining my normal routine much harder.

Long hair and drugs and rock music were in full swing at this time and I threw myself with reckless abandon into that world much to the dismay of my befuddled father. Looking back I'm sure he had a difficult time relating to a son with long hair and coming and going with friends who were not all that neat in appearance. A scruffy lot we all were, and that was on our good days. We went out of our way to shock people with our hair and unkempt look. We reveled in that.

Getting high was not just for weekends now – hey – it was okay to do during the day, even when I was at school. I was stoned on something different everyday it seemed. Inside I wanted my dad to notice, to see I was a mess. I don't think he did, and if he did notice he didn't know how to handle it. My bad behavior was my way of screaming to my father: PLEASE NOTICE ME! PLEASE HAVE A RELATIONSHIP WITH ME! I would find out later, my messaging was not understood by my dad.

One day I decided to go to see one of the high school counselors in our school about my desire to have a closer relationship with my father. That was my first experience with a professional counselor and it was a total disaster as far as I was concerned.

I walked into the counselor's office, and began to tell her about my relationship with my father; and how I wanted him to be more involved with me – with my life. I was very emotional and had tears in my eyes; but I soon realized the person staring back at me was showing no empathy or sympathy; at least that's how it seemed.

By the reaction of the counselor, or actually the lack of response; I realized I might as well have been talking to the mirror on the wall! The counselor defended my father's behavior and left me feeling like the entire problem between my father and me was my fault.

I left completely depressed, and convinced that going to see a counselor was one of the worst ideas I've ever had. To my knowledge, the counselor made no attempt to contact my father to try and reconcile our differences. Let me simply say that for me at that time of my life – counseling was not only not helpful – it made matters much worse.

After that experience, I felt more alone and separated from my father than at any other time in my life. I didn't hate or despise my dad, not hardly; I just wanted him to be more interested in me and more involved with my life as his son.

That was not to be. From the day I walked out of that counselor's office; I had this terrible feeling that things between my father and me were going to get much worse. Now I felt the only way to get my father's attention, to get him involved with me was to act up – and that's exactly what I did.

Sadly, my life was going in a downward spiral very quickly, and I was skipping school more and more. Somehow I managed to get passing grades without much effort, and I was on my way to graduating needing only one credit by the time I reached my senior year of high school.

In my final year of high school things got really crazy and I was desperately wanting to have a relationship with my father. He seemed oblivious to me, and that was driving me to act more and more erratic in an attempt to get his attention – to get any kind of reaction out of him! I didn't care if he screamed at me, I just wanted him to be in my life – to notice me.

It all came to a head, when I was kicked out of school for three days for missing too many days of school. The principal called me into the office and informed me that I was being expelled for 3 days because of my poor attendance. I was told I had missed 22 half days for that semester.

I wanted to shock my dad into doing something, anything just to get him to be involved with my life. At this point our relationship was basically non existent; we would say a few words to each other occasionally – and even then it was very superficial. Surely I reasoned to myself, this time my dad will have to talk to me – he'll have to get involved in my life.

I was wrong!

I had to go home that day and inform my dad that I was kicked out of school for 3 days, which I dreaded as any teenage boy would in those circumstances... I decided to go for broke. I was going to shock my father into action, into being involved with my life even if it was over something stupid and reprehensible. I decided to concoct a story so outrageous that surely he would get involved with me, with my problems, with my unhappy life!

I went home and told my father that I had been expelled from school for the entire year! I thought to myself, "he's going to call the school" - "he's going to find out what happened", and get involved with me.

To my surprise, he believed me hook, line and sinker. He didn't even bother to call the school to check my story, or try to find out what was going on. That blew my mind totally.

My father became furious, and told me I had two days to find a job, and said some other things in anger that I don't remember because at the time I was in a state of unbelief – that my father was that uncaring and insensitive to not even bother to call the school about my situation.

I was hurt beyond words, and got up to begin looking for a job that I knew I wasn't going to be able to find. This was another one of my worst "bad days", just like the day my mother had her nervous breakdown. Only this day was worse. This was the beginning of a very zany and wild journey I was about to embark upon – and I was barely seventeen at the time.

Today, if that were to happen – I would probably "fess up" and tell my dad the truth - "Hey dad, I just want to see if you cared enough to call the principal." Or, I just might say "evict me", I'm not going anywhere! I've heard teens today are much more likely to pull that on their parents then "self destruct" like I did...

The reality at that time was simple. I was too angry to let my dad know what the truth was; and at the same time I did have respect for his authority as my father. Looking back later; I realized that I was just a mixed up young man, who was desperate to have a relationship with his father. As we all know we can't turn back time, that's only in the movies.

I learned much later, that relationships between people are always there, it's just a matter of "what kind of relationship." Our relationship was cool and distant, with little affection or personal intimacy that one normally associates with a healthy "father and son" relationship...

Okay, I admit it – I went about it all wrong; and in the process I actually sabotaged our relationship to the point that I was now seriously estranged from my dad in the worst possible way. I can't say I hated him; but I was extremely upset and hurt by that episode of my teen years.

It would be a few years later, before I would finally forgive my dad for what I perceived was the ultimate betrayal from a father to his own son. The pain was deep, and it was something that I would struggle with deep within my soul as the next few years unfolded.

I can say at that time, my father and I had no further communication for years... as far as I was concerned he was dead. When you're seventeen, you don't have life figured out, and in my mind (though my perception was not accurate); my father had done the unforgivable.

My father was kicking me out of the house! It was my fault for lying to my dad, which resulted in him over reacting; which resulted in me being on the street homeless. That was true, but at seventeen, and emotionally unstable at that time; I felt justified in holding my father responsible for making me leave home. I left home an angry and bitter young man.

Legally at the time, he couldn't force me to leave home; but that never entered my mind. Besides – my stubborn pride, and my pent up anger towards my father was such that I didn't want to stay with him anymore. I would show him, I could make it on my own – I could survive – I could and would not be back. It's funny how easy decisions are made in the thick of our most intense emotions.

We learn later, that decisions made in haste or while in a state of raw emotion usually end up with disastrous results. Boy o boy, that certainly was true in my case – and I wouldn't have to wait very long to have serious regrets about my decision to go along with my dad's forced exodus of myself from our home.

This was to be the end of our relationship as father and son, and I determined that under no circumstances would I ever live with my father again. That proved to be true; and I would in fact never live with my dad again – not for one day, not ever. That was my view of our relationship at the time; and I never really found out what my father thought of that whole depressing episode between me and him .

There was a popular Motown song out at the time: Only The Strong Survive[6], by Jerry Butler; who also toured with the group "The Impressions." That song was my theme song, or anthem for the next few years. I can't remember how many times I would sing the line, "Only the strong survive," whenever I found myself in dire circumstances...

Funny how a simple song can give you strength when you're feeling weak or lonely; such is the power and sway of music and words over our emotions. I know it did with me... There were other songs, but that song in particular held some kind of unusual connection to me in the days that would follow.

My life was about to go from a somewhat normal suburban existence – to a crazy unpredictable journey from Michigan to California. My best friend at the time, Jerry LeBloch decided to hitch-hike to the West Coast with me, and I can say neither of us were prepared for the long journey before us.

At this point in my story, I think some honest reflection is necessary. I'm quite certain that had my best friend at the time, Jerry not agreed to go with me; I probably wouldn't have tried to head out to California by myself. Maybe – but probably not. It's truly amazing how things happen in our lives that can totally change the outcome of "what might have been?"

That Jerry did agree to go with me, and that without me having to talk him into it – is quite remarkable when I look back at those zany days. Now I realize that the odds of getting a friend, any friend to just get up and thumb it across the US with practically nothing - is slim to none.

The next part of my bizarre journey as a naive young teenager, with no real clue about how bad and terrifying this world can be when you are out on your own; was bearable because when you are with a friend things don't seem so bad. There is something good to be said about friends going through hard times together. Jerry & I were not alone – and that was good.

Jerry & me / summer of 1967

Jerry LeBloch was my best friend at that time – and kindred spirits in so many ways... At that time – our hair was considered very long and a sign of rebellion. I was not allowed to have my senior pictures taken and we were called: Kikes We wore that title like a "badge of honor!"

THUMBING IT TO CALIFORNIA

...that you may be sons of your Father in heaven; for He makes His sun rise on the evil and on the good, and sends rain on the just and on the unjust.
Mt.5:45

Being barely seventeen, and knowing little about how scary the world can be, my naivete at that time was really a blessing. I was young and dumb and living on pure emotions more than anything. I was angry at my father, really angry – and that somehow drove me on hour by hour. I didn't know what I was going to do – but I was sure of one thing. I was not going to crawl back to my father and beg him to let me stay at home.

I was an angry young man, hurt and confused. It wouldn't be until years later that I realized how foolish and brash my behavior was during that time of my life. It would also be years later that I would realize that God was watching over me, and was there all the time, even when my whole world seemed like it was crashing down on me!

The next few months, there would be lots of "rain" and there would also be plenty of "sunshine" that I would experience, and it would deeply affect me in ways that I could never have imagined at that painful period of my life.

I spent a full day looking for a job, actually going from store to store, business to business asking if I could get a job, or if they were hiring?

I got some funny looks, and some pitiful glances, but as I had expected my chances of getting a job at the tender age of 17 were slim to none. (I had just turned 17 that month)

Sure I was scared, but there was no way I was going to tell my father the truth about my only being expelled for three days, and not the entire year like I had told him. Hurt and angry, I started coming to grips with the reality that I wasn't going to find a job in two days – I was not sure what I would do next?

I knew lying to my father was wrong – but I honestly never imagined that he would react by throwing me out of the house! It was too late to undo what I had started – too late to turn back now, my stubborn pride wouldn't allow for that...

My best friend at the time, Jerry LeBloch[2] was living in an unhappy home at the time with his father, and I thought maybe, just maybe Jerry might want to leave home with me and hitch-hike to California.

Jerry and his father were having problems, and Jerry's long hair was a point of major contention at that time. It turns out that Jerry's long hair and my problem with my father were all falling in line at the same time.

I called Jerry up and told him about my situation, and about my idea of heading out west; and to my delight Jerry was keen on the prospect of thumbing it to California with me. I felt relieved knowing that I wasn't alone in my misery. It is true - "misery loves company."

It's worth pointing out at this juncture, that Jerry LeBloch and I were band mates, and our first band The Mid-Nite Sonz, was a basement band to be sure. We played a few small gigs around the area at that time, but we were a long way from being sought after by major labels looking for bands to sign. Playing music together was exciting and we were hooked.

At that point in our musical journey, we didn't even have a bass guitar in the mix. One of us would strum the rhythm guitar on the bass notes to make up for no bass, and the drummer (Jerry), would have to work a little harder to fill in the weak spots. Somehow it sounded pretty good, but looking back it was definitely a weakness for us a band.

Even back then Jerry could do a nice drum solo, that would only get better as Jerry progressed as a world class drummer. We would do the song Wipe Out, and at some point Jerry would just take off and then we would jump back in for the rest of the song to the end. Those were some good times!Left to right/Pat Sharp – lead guitar/Drums – Jerry Le Bloch Me – rhythm guitar/vocals – far right ?

That's me in Jerry's basement playing the harmonica

**Left to right/Pat Sharp – lead guitar / Drums – Jerry LeBloch & me
-rhythm guitar/vocals - and Jim Bissonette ? (**he was auditioning for the
band)

We had plenty of passion, and tons of energy that drove our parents crazy I'm sure. We made a lot of noise, and for us the louder it was the better! Rock and roll music was in our blood, and we were smitten.

Guitars, long hair, girls, and anything to do with rock music and bands filled our hearts and minds at that time. I can say that playing music was the only time I really felt like I could escape the negative things going on in my own life – it was an escape for both of us. We would jam at my home or Jerry's home, and that became a type of "high" that we never seemed to get enough of...

The English bands were in full bloom, with bands like the Beatles and The Rolling Stones, paving the way for American bands to follow in their footsteps... I can say that both of us spent most of our free time listening to all the new bands that were on the radio and T.V. at that time.

Jerry went on to become a world class drummer, touring with bands like Rare Earth, "The Drifters", The Platters, Dick Wagner; and many others during his long and successful career as a premier rock and roll drummer.

Leaving our suburban homes where we had a fairly comfortable life as middle class teens; and then going off half broke hitch -hiking across the country would mean putting our love and dream of being "rock stars" on hold – at least for a while.

13 Dollars & A Duffel Bag

On the 2nd day of my expulsion from school, Jerry and I put our plan together for leaving our homes and heading out west. We scrounged up 13 dollars and a few packs of cigarettes, a few t-shirts, some blue jeans, and stuffed that and a few other personal belongings into a canvas duffel bag.

Being young and naive has it's advantages as we were more excited about our sojourn to California and the adventure we were about to embark upon – than any fears of the unknown that may have been in the back of our minds...

We were apprehensive for sure, but we had each other to share this trip together; and we knew that we both needed a change. I didn't realize how much I was about to change in the next few months, but changes were coming, and coming in spades...

One thing I can tell you is this: you grow up very fast when you are living on the street, on the road; not knowing where you're going to sleep or what you're going to eat from day to day. Yes sir, you grow up real fast! I can honestly say that I learned more about life and survival during the next six months of living on the road than I had in all sixteen years prior to going out west...

There are only two things on your mind when your seventeen and hitch-hiking across the country with only a few dollars and a bag containing everything you own. Where am I going to sleep tonight, and what am I going to eat today? Really, life becomes very simple, and focused. O yeah, and one other thing: Be on guard for perverts, and weirdos that might do something really really bad to you! (that was always on our minds)

We managed to get a ride most of the time without much difficulty; and that was probably because we looked so young and pitiful... we hadn't been on our own long enough to look scary, just like two young guys with long hair heading out west.

Keep in mind, that at that time, hitch-hiking was very common – in fact it wasn't unusual to find five or six people in the same place with cardboard signs; all going somewhere by thumbing it. It was perfectly normal and we were probably more frightened at the prospect of being picked up by a crazy pervert than the motorists were of us. One thing was for sure, you never knew who was going to be giving you a ride next? Straight people, stoned out hippies, truckers, - hey and sometimes even a ride in a police car! (More on that later)

Begging And Handouts

It didn't take long for our 13 dollars to vanish, and we now began asking for help, money or whatever anyone could spare to make it through each day. I had never had to beg anyone before in my life for anything; but found it wasn't hard to do when your belly is empty and your dirty and scared and a long way from home. You do what you have to do to survive.

I remember asking for money from strangers walking down the street, and telling them that we were hungry and from Michigan and just wanted help so we could get something to eat.

Many people would hand us a dollar or two, usually without making eye contact and we would thank them and wait for the next person to come by to beg them for money.

Somehow, we managed to find a place to sleep and at least something to eat each day; though we both were shedding pounds with each passing week. Some people would take us to a restaurant or buy us a meal, and some kind souls would let us sleep in their vehicle or allow us to stay in their home for a day or longer in some cases. We learned to live on candy bars, and junk food, and whatever we could scrounge up for that day.

We had been living in California now for months, and had become street wise from having to beg, borrow, steal, or con anyone we could to make it to the next day. Survival is the name of the game when you're living on the road day by day; and you learn not to trust anyone, but hope that everyone will trust you.

I remember missing things like being able to take a hot shower, or crawling into my own bed for a good night's sleep. Just walking to the fridge and grabbing a snack was something that I would never take for granted again if and when I ever got into my own place.

Another thing that became a real pain, was always having to find a public bathroom where we could take care of our personal business and clean up. But, perhaps the biggest difficulty we faced was having no money.

That was a constant reminder of how needy we really were, and we were very needy! Being broke is something you can get used to, but it is never fun.

As crazy as it may sound(even with the negative things I just mentioned), being young and dumb has it's benefits. It didn't really bother us to be homeless, penniless, and hungry, or dirty(not that I enjoyed it); but we actually thought we were living the life!

Being long haired hippies, living day to day was an adventure – and somehow we managed to see the "glass as half full" - which I largely attribute to our naivete about life; and our being high on something most of the time.

Hey, we had no one to answer to, no one to tell us what to do, we were happy living as vagabonds without any real goal other than getting through one more day, and finding someone to get high with – and some food and a place to sleep. We were young and dumb and loving it – well, most of it. But, keep in mind that this was the period of free love, peace, and being "hippies" had a strange appeal to us at that time of our lives...

Though much of that time hitch -hiking across the country is now a big blurry memory; I do remember some things clearly. That's probably because of the fact that many of those experiences were "first time" events in my life.

We all remember our first time breaking a bone, or perhaps our first kiss, or first fight... my point being many of the things that happened to us were once in a life time experiences, or at the very least – our first time experiencing them. Hitch-hiking to California one one of those events.

The number one thing that always remained constant was this: Keep moving, keep going – we couldn't stop long anywhere because we had no place to go to! We had no idea of where we were going to end up(other than the state of California). That short term agenda of "getting to California" kept us focused; but would soon end; and leave us wondering...

What do we do now that we're here?

When you're a teenager miles from home, and lacking any worldly sophistication; you simply don't think too far beyond what your going through at the moment. As they say, ignorance is bliss... We were certainly ignorant of a lot of things, and yes – we were most definitely "blissful"...

Were we scared? Yes, sometimes. Were we cold and hungry? Too many times to keep straight. But, and this is the funny part. We honestly were having the time of our lives. Really. We were meeting new people everyday(every hour actually); and we were finally able to grow our hair out as long as we wanted without anyone making us cut it or pull it back out of sight...

Having long hair these days is not so popular, "beards" and a few days of managed stubble is more the craze with guys of all ages it seems. But at the time Jerry & I were on the road; being able to grow your hair long, past your shoulders was a big cultural ritual for teens pushing the norms.

It was something that separated us from the "straight" and boring adults and peers that were against the world of rock music, drugs, and experimentation that was at the center of everything many young people were immersed in at that time.

We were young and dumb, but having the adventure of our lives and loving almost, I said, "almost every minute of it!" That being said, I must admit once should have been enough for me; but a year later I hitch-hiked out west again with another friend - Jim Thorpe. (He died years later in a tragic fire in Florida) Jim later opened a record store in Flint, Michigan and was the most knowledgeable person I've ever know when it came to knowing every possible bit of trivia about The Beatles(who he idolized), as well as most rock-&-roll bands period. The guy was simply amazing!

Unfortunately for Jim, I had made the mistake of making my first trip out west by thumb sound like a fun-filled adventure (which in part it was); but truthfully it was mostly a hard core encounter of long days of being hungry, cold, and afraid! Scared of who and what was up ahead at the next town or rest stop; and always wondering where we would end up sleeping at the day's end. Looking back – I feel bad for talking Jim into going on that second trip to California... that proved to be a big mistake for both of us.

That being said, I have to say I got to travel out west with 2 of my best friends and in spite of the all the negatives we experienced, what didn't kill us most certainly made us stronger as the old adage goes. Jerry & Jim are both gone now, but the memories I have of our time together thumbing down highways will always be with me until I cross over to the other side.

My first trip out west with Jerry LeBloch, was a dream compared to my 2nd trip out west with Jim Thorpe. All I will say at this time is I should never have hitch-hiked to California a second time... it was a total disaster in every way. I should have known better, but it was only when I was thousands of miles away from Michigan that I realized what a horrible mistake I had made doing this "living by the thumb" thing over again.

And just for the record, I never did hitch to California a third time. Now back to where Jerry and I were on our crazy trip thumbing across the U.S.

THE FREE LOVE GENERATION[8]

Everyone seemed to be doing drugs at that time, at least most of the people we would run into or stay with. This was the "love, peace, and rock-and-roll" generation; and we were in the thick of it. We would get high on a regular basis with hippies and weekend warriors whenever we could, and drugs were in ample supply – whatever you wanted.

We usually were given drugs for free, LSD, marijuana, hash – or sometimes offered a beer or alcohol; because "turning someone" on to a new drug, or just sharing your drugs and alcohol with others was considered the social norm at that time. Sharing your drugs was just expected.

This meant we never really went very long without getting high, which numbed our senses and helped us deal with the stress of not knowing where we would sleep or what we would eat that day. When you're stoned – you don't worry, you just live in that moment – that hour. Drugs became a sedative, a means of coping with our ever changing environment.

We experimented with lots of LSD, and other hallucinogenic drugs, and of course when you don't have your own car or home or place to retreat to – things can get very scary and bizarre. That's what started to happen to us. Being high all of the time, being broke, and hungry and dirty started to take it's toll on both of us and we started thinking about going back to Michigan.

By this time we were tired of living on the street, and living off the charity of strangers; we began to plan our exodus from California back to our home state of Michigan. At this time we had been living on the road for about six months.

A Kind Christian Woman

Before I share about our return to Michigan after living as hippies and wanderers for six months, I think it's only fitting that I mention a few encounters with Christians and Jesus freaks that left an indelible impression on both of us.

I can't remember what state we were in, or what day it was; but I do remember what happened to us on a cold day somewhere out in the middle of nowhere. Again, what city or town I can't recall, but I do know we stopped at a truck-stop to clean up and get something to eat before we started thumbing our way down the road again to our next destination – wherever that might be. I lost track of all the places we stopped at, to me it was just another stop along the way.

A kind woman, with a soft voice started talking to us about where we were going, where we had come from; and other questions like that. After talking to her for a short time she revealed to us that she was the owner of the truck-stop, and also a Christian. It's funny that I can't remember what she looked like – but I do remember she seemed very interested in our pitiful situation.

She asked if she could pray for us, and she took us into her office in the back and shared some scriptures with us(what I can't remember); and she prayed with us. Before we got up to leave she gave us some money, I think it was around twenty dollars, and told us that she would be praying for us.

That kind of thing happened to us more than once, and we always knew that God was there, somehow behind the scenes moving through people's kindness and generosity to help us and take care of us. I'll always remember that woman, and wish I could remember her name, and who she was so I could thank her for her act of kindness to two young men who were just strangers to her.

Her small act of compassion to us made a difference in our lives that day. This kind woman who's name I can't remember, is a reminder of all of the noble and kindhearted persons in the Bible, who's names were never divulged. Our lives are touched in big and small ways by people God brings across our path; and often we are unaware of how God is using them to show His grace and mercy to us.

This woman at the truck-stop; is someone I expect to meet in heaven one day – at least I hope so.

Jesus Freaks[9]

Another strange encounter occurred in Laguna Beach, California; when we were out on the street panhandling and hustling people for money and a place to sleep for that evening.

This time, it was a bunch of Jesus people, or Jesus freaks as most people called them back then - that we ran into. We were out begging for food or money, and we saw a group of young people who seemed very excited and happy about something. They were "witnessing" to people on the street about Jesus Christ.

I didn't know anything about these kind of Christians, my entire background and experience with Christianity was based on my experience with the Catholic church, and my understanding of traditional Christians. By that I mean, getting dressed up and going to church on Sunday, and being very straight laced and conservative in appearance and manners.

These young people were anything but that. They had on holy blue jeans, tie dyed t-shirts, headbands, and looked pretty much like us; except they were clean and they looked a lot happier and together than we did – that's for sure. They talked to us about the Bible, about Jesus Christ, and about their own relationships with God, and other things concerning Christianity.

To be honest we just wanted a place to sleep for that evening, and some food; so we asked them if they could help us. They made us a proposal. If we would come and listen to a Bible study with them, then afterwards they would feed us, and we could sleep there for the night. That sounded reasonable, and off we went to our first Bible study with these Jesus freaks that we had just met.

I don't remember what they shared out of the Bible, but I do remember they were all kind and very sincere in their witnessing to us. I wasn't sure what to think of their message that day; but I was impressed by how much love and genuine compassion they were showing us. A seed was planted in our hearts that day by these young Christians who were not like anyone that I had come to associate with Christianity.

The next morning after being fed again, and getting a decent night's sleep we were introduced to our first "let's hold hands" prayer meeting... that was a strange, very strange event for me – and has never left my memory ever since.

I remember holding hands with about ten to twelve of these Jesus freaks, and each of them praying out loud prayers that they seemed to be speaking out spontaneously. Then I heard what sounded like foreign languages being spoken, but I had no idea whatsoever what language or tongue they were speaking. Somehow, I just knew that they were speaking a language from God – from heaven. These Christians were indeed "freaks", even to me, a young man who was not easily freaked out.

For once, Jerry and I were on the other side of being "freaked out."

It wasn't until years later that I discovered that these young Jesus people were praying in "tongues"(2), a gift of the Holy Spirit that allows individuals to speak in other tongues - languages as the Spirit gives that person the ability to speak.

We didn't become Christians that day, or pray for salvation or anything that bold or drastic; but we did pray with them and allow them to pray for us. One thing is certain, when I left that place I would never forget the "holy presence" we felt when we were with them. God once again had planted seed in our hearts, and was there letting us know He was taking care of us and watching over us.

There were many occasions like this where we knew God was using people, sometimes Christians – and sometimes not; but we always had this sense that we were going to be okay – that God was with us. Now I know that someone, somewhere must have been praying for us.

Sometimes we experience things in life that let you know, someone – somewhere is thinking about you. Well, we had just such an experience while we were living in Laguna Beach, California just prior to our decision to return to Michigan.

The band The Frost, whom Jerry and I had been roadies for in Michigan for a short time had just released a new album: THE FROST, on Vanguard Records. So, we decided we would purchase it and listen to their new songs. What we heard floored us.

They had a goofy song about "groupies", the girls that hung around bands for attention and any action they might find before,during and after band performances. Anyways – near the end of the song: "Little Susy Singer", we hear the lyrics: "D'Aigle and LeBloch – where are you?"

Wow! We were absolutely blown away by that! The Frost was looking for us, they actually put out that message on their latest record – just to let us know – Hey you guys "we miss you – come on back home."

We knew right then and there, we had to head back to Michigan. It made us feel good to know someone, this band we had worked for and become friends with – was actually thinking about us! Aw – it made us feel all warm and fuzzy; and we felt like we were loved and missed. That was something neither of us was feeling from our families back home.

It wasn't long after that, that we packed up our few belongings and headed back to our home state of Michigan. We were enjoying California, and all the crazy antics and people that we were surrounded by everyday. But, in our hearts we sensed it was time to say goodbye to the West Coast and head on back to our friends and home town.

I don't remember if we had any money when we left California to come back home, but if we did it wasn't much. We never worked while we were on the road hitch-hiking, and spent most of our time getting stoned on whatever we could and trying to have fun when and wherever we could.

Most moms would have called us bums; and I have to admit that's what we were. We had collected a number of souvenirs and mementos to bring back with us from Haight Ashbury, and other places around California.

Posters, incense, and other things we had managed to get a hold of or steal or connive someone out of were now on there way back to Michigan with us. They were proof to our friends and others that we had been where we said we were, and "badges of honor" to both of us...

Oh, and did I almost forget to mention that we had some psychedelic drugs we were bringing back with us, though we were careful to hide them just in case we were stopped by the police.

Sure enough, we would be stopped by the police, and most of the things we were bringing back would not make it back with us. We were both about to find out how small we were in a big world where two teenage young men are essentially at the mercy of anyone bigger or with more authority than us. That was just about everyone.

What happened next to me personally, would change forever the way I felt about things like, "civil rights", "police brutality" and "injustice." Our trip back to Michigan was uneventful, which when you're hitching cross country is not a bad thing; it simply means you're not being threatened or propositioned by some weirdo – or something far worse.

But, just as we were nearing the Southern boarder of Michigan at the Ohio/Michigan state line; our trip was about to become something that you see in movies. Not the happy, or humorous scenes; but rather the scenes that make you wince or simply glad you're not actually living the drama before you on the screen.

The problem was, what happened to us was not a dream, and it was for me worse than any nightmare I've had in my life. We knew were just 2 guys drifting along; not rich or powerful by anyone's standards; but we were young and cocky and not easily intimidated. That was misguided confidence, and was about to be shattered by what we both were about to experience.

A NIGHTMARE IN LIMA, OHIO

All of us have memorable events in our lives. Most of them we don't remember; but the ones that stand out and that we do remember usually have strong emotions attached to them. I believe that is why psychologists say we remember some things so vividly. Like the time when you were in a car accident, or when you were in a fight in the schoolyard where you lost your front teeth. Or the time when your father gave you a spanking because you were caught stealing money out of your parent's top dresser drawer. Those kind of things never leave us.

One such memory has never left me, and still brings back terrible thoughts and emotions whenever I think about it. It happened as Jerry and I were making our way back to Michigan, after being out west for six months living hand to mouth as homeless drifters.

We were arrested by two young Ohio State troopers; who charged us with: Taking up space on a public highway. (That's another way of saying we weren't supposed to be standing there) That was the beginning of my personal nightmare in Lima, Ohio.

They arrested us on some minor infraction which was basically because we were vagrants and not supposed to be hitch-hiking where we were along the highway. I had this terrible feeling that this was going to be a bad day. I was right, it ended up being one of the worst days of my life!

I was still seventeen so I was put in the county jail, Jerry was nineteen, so they put him in the city jail. Jerry was let out within 24 hours and thumbed it back to Michigan, while I was not so fortunate. I was never allowed to make a phone call or see a lawyer or told that I had any rights.

We were all alone, with no money, and finding out that Lima , Ohio was not a good place to be for a long haired boys from Michigan...

My souvenirs my coat, my belongings and personal effects were all taken from me or destroyed. To say I was scared would be a gross understatement – I was truly horrified to discover that I was locked up in a dirty jail somewhere in Ohio, and no one knew where I was, no one but my friend Jerry and I didn't know where he was or if he was still locked up like me.

I spent seven horrible, long, tiring days in jail in Lima Ohio; and was never allowed to call home, or for that matter to take a shower. I found out just how pitifully unimportant I was - just a long haired young man, alone and with no one to help me out of this sorry predicament I was in. Or so it seemed.

Knowing that no one knew where I was, and that I was destitute with no money, left me in the regrettable position of being literally a "nobody" as far as the Lima police were concerned. I was seriously concerned about my safety, and began wondering what my fate might be? When your seventeen, alone, and have never been in jail a day in you life – your imagination under those circumstances begins to go off into the dark deep end.

Mine did.

I had no idea what had become of my friend Jerry, and they hadn't told me anything. In fact, they treated me with the utmost contempt, and never allowed me to shower or brush my teeth, or have any soap to cleanse myself. They kept threatening to cut my hair(which was quite long), and I began to really think I might be spending a long, long time in this rotten jail in Lima, Ohio.

When you're in a cell with nothing but the four walls, and a metal frame to sleep on (they didn't provide me with a mattress), you spend a lot of time just walking back and forth... that and thinking – thinking about anything and everything. I began to look at the idea of being "bored to death" in a entirely new way.

I hate to admit it but at that time I was addicted to nicotine, and I began tearing out the pages of a small New Testament, and actually smoking them after I rolled them up. That was something I now regret. Just stupid.

Free As A Bird

My friend Jerry, who was put in another jail because he was older(he was nineteen), had been released and had thumbed his way back home to Flint, Michigan. He told my parents where I was, and they sent ten dollars to put me on a bus back home.

The day I was supposed to have all my hair cut off, was the day they released me. It has to be one of the best days of my entire life, and the feeling of being let out of that hell hole of misery can only be described as pure delight from head to toe! I can still remember the joy in my heart at knowing I was being set free – freedom! Freedom! It tasted sweet, very sweet and delicious to my soul.

I have to say at this point that this experience affected me in ways that I still carry with me today. I learned that injustice is alive and well in our country, and that being alone, and without money can be very dangerous. It has made me very compassionate towards those who are in jail or in prison; and slow to pass judgment on them as well.

God only knows how many young men and women have been denied their civil rights, and worse; at the hands of those in authority who were supposed to be protecting and guarding those who are most vulnerable and helpless.

Being locked up , and treated with such contempt and disregard for my civil rights and my dignity as a human being– changed my perspective on life forever. It didn't harden me, but it did make me more cynical and less trusting of those in authority – especially those in law enforcement.

One thing was certain, my nearly six months of living on the road, day to day without knowing where my next meal was going to come from; or where I was going to sleep – had changed me forever! I was not the young naive clueless lad that had left Michigan just months earlier. As I said before, you grow up fast when your survival is on the line – yep – and I grew up really fast.

Finally, I was on my way home, on a bus taking me back to Flint Michigan; but once again I found myself thinking: "Where will I go when I get back? Where will I sleep? What will I eat?" I was excited about going back to familiar surroundings and old friends, but scared that in truth – I had no place to go. The sad truth was I was going back to Michigan – but to what?

I'm A Hippie

There were two groups of people that I associated with at this time of my life and they were both very much alike. The first group were what we called: Weekend Warriors. These were mostly young guys and girls that liked to party hearty as we used to say. But when the party was over they would all head back home to their nice homes in the suburbs or uptown.

The other group were the "hippies", who didn't have a nice home to go back to when the party was over. This group were 24/7 dopers and freaks as we would refer to ourselves. I was in this group at this time of my life.

To survive we would find a home, and just about any home would do. We would pool our meager resources together and live together as a commune of sorts and live day to day with little concern other than staying warm and having a little something in the fridge to eat.

So after returning to Michigan, I lived as a hippie, and spent my time playing guitar, or going to different parties whenever or wherever that happened to be on any given day.

Life was very simple: Get high, find some drugs and people to get high with and look for a party to go to that evening. Our daily routine was predictable and to the left of center.

All this time I was slowly beginning to realize that doing drugs, and hanging out with stoned out people was getting old – getting very boring ; and I was wondering how I might climb out of this dead end street I was stuck in? I managed to avoid doing heroin, though some of my friends were experimenting with it. The likelihood of me eventually trying it myself, and getting hooked was a very real possibility.

I said I would never smoke cigarettes, and at that time I was smoking a pack a day; so if good intentions couldn't keep me from nicotine – they probably wouldn't keep me from heroin either.

It's worth pointing out that I never felt sorry for myself, though I did resent my father for kicking me out of our home when I was only seventeen. My anger towards my father motivated me to carry on no matter what. I was determined to never ask my father to help me again – somehow no matter how bad things might get I made up my mind I would not go back home – not ever! I was an angry young man filled with stubborn pride!

Strangely, my life was about to go from the drug houses of Flint to the Holiday Inns of America – all in one day! One day I was just sitting around with some other hippies in a dope house in Flint, Michigan when in walks my old hitch-hiking buddy Jerry with a grin on his face and an invitation I just couldn't refuse.

Before I share the crazy – zany life that I was about to embark on let me say that my life as a bona fide hippie was beginning to lose any appeal that it once had on me. I was more than ready for a change ; for something positive to happen. Hanging out with stoned out drug addicts and some of the weirdest people you could ever meet; had me wondering just where my life was going?

To be honest – no where! Or as I discovered later – I was on my way to hell and just caught up in a life of living day to day with no real goals or plans for my future. It's amazing how little we can settle for when we are just living for self, when we are just looking for something or someone to give us momentary pleasure.

My life was about to change, that was for sure – but what started out very positive in the beginning would eventually take me even further into a world of darkness and despair. Having hitched across the U.S. with Jerry I knew it couldn't be any worse than that; besides Jerry painted a rosy picture of what my life was going to be like if I chose to join him.

THE BIG TIME!

I remember Jerry telling me that a band, <u>THE FROST</u>, with Dick Wagner[2], were going on tour out west, and he wanted to know if I wanted to go and work as a roadie with him? Having no job, no money, and nothing going on in my life at that time the decision took me all of one nano second to say, "yes" - when do we leave?

I went from living in a dope house with a bunch of hippies, doing nothing from day to day – to life in the "fast lane". Jerry and I had worked with this band before, but now they had hit the big time, and were going on tour to both the East and West coasts. Life all of a sudden got really crazy, and I was more than ready for a change.

Now within days I would be on tour on the east coast and the west coast with one of the top bands at that time, and I was in a state of bliss at this turn of events. Suddenly I was in the Big Time, at least in my mind that's for sure.

Amazingly, only a few months earlier I was penniless, homeless, and living on the streets – with my hitch-hiking buddy, *Jerry Lebloch; and now I'm going to be hanging out with some of the richest and most famous rock stars in the world. This new adventure was going to blow my mind in more ways than one!

Jerry and I now had our own apartment, a van to call our own, a weekly salary, and best of all we were doing something we both loved – immersed in rock music and hanging around people like us who were at the top of their game. We were in the big time and loving every minute of it. Our apartment was in Saginaw, Michigan where the FROST were based out of.

Our job as Road Managers, was making sure the band had everything they needed for their concerts and festival engagements. Packing and unpacking their band equipment and setting it up was our main task, but we did a multitude of other things for them from taking clothes to the cleaners, to changing guitar strings if needed at gigs... we did whatever had to be done to make things run smoothly.

It's amazing how easy it was for me to adjust from living with a bunch of stoned out hippies in a dope house in Flint – to having money, an apartment, clothes and an entirely new world full of adventure and things I loved – girls, rock music, and more drugs – life in the "fast lane."

This was in stark contrast to my harsh adjustment in learning how to live hand to mouth hitch-hiking across America. I was now living a dream life, or so I thought when it all began...

Drugs, Sex, & Rock-and-Roll

One thing that didn't change was the drugs. I was still using drugs, only now I had more money to buy drugs with - better drugs and more of them(actually I should I say "worse" drugs)   Also, sex and rock and roll were the only things that seemed to matter to me, so my life was centered around those three things. I was happy at the time, life seemed good – and I was having fun. It's true there is pleasure in sin...

The irony is that while I now had more money and a nice place to live in, cool clothes and plenty of girls to be with – I was still doing the same things I was doing when I was broke, and homeless – just that now I was doing it in excess and in the comfort of Holiday Inns, and with rich and famous rock stars.

The stories you've heard about the groupies and orgies and all the excesses that are associated with the rock and roll music business are real – they are for the most part true. I avoided some of that, but with everyone pushing the boundaries it was hard to say "no" I won't do that.

The bottom line during that period of my life was this: It was hard to say no to all the temptations, when I was living in the thick of it. It was very easy to say "yes" to whatever sin or vice was presented to me because it was always there – always available. Living a godly and virtuous life was not high on my list of priorities at that time of my life; and it was obviously not what was going on all around me.

In my mind, I was not a bad person, I was just doing what everyone else around me was doing - and now doing it with style. Jerry and I had our own house, new clothes, new friends, an exciting life going from one concert to the next. Girls, drugs, rock -and-roll everyday – I really thought life couldn't get any better.

Finding girls who wanted to be associated with a popular rock band was an added benefit; and admittedly I took advantage of that fact whenever I could. There were lots of fringe benefits to being Roadies for a successful band like The Frost. It seemed that everyone wanted to be on the "inside" of the action we were part of. Friends were easy to find when you were connected to a big time band. That's just the way the music world works.

I cannot over emphasize how my life from being a pauper with nothing but a few personal belongings, to my new found status as a Roadie for a touring successful band/The Frost affected me. This new life was a huge boost to my down-and-out psyche that only months earlier had me feeling like a nobody. For at least a short time, I was truly happy inside and living like I was in someone's dream.

We were living in the fast lane and loving it! Admittedly, my love for the world and it's pleasures had me in it's spell. While satisfying my daily lusts and desires consumed most of my thoughts – I knew deep in my heart there was more to life than that. Finding out what that was – that would take some time, and miles and miles of twists and turns.

BACKSTAGE WITH THE STARS

Things sure look different backstage... The audience comes to concerts expecting a show – lights, smoke, special effects – and that's what they usually see and experience. Ah – but being with a band, before/during/and after the concert gives you a different perspective . Let me say right here that much if it isn't very pretty – it can gross a rank sinner out; I know because it did me!

I cannot speak openly of the things I saw and heard, and even did myself here in this book. It would make this book x-rated. So I'll simply relate some of what I witnessed and took part in as nicely as I can without being too graphic or offensive..

Getting used to being around rich and famous rock stars took me a while to get used to – but after months of being backstage with some of the biggest names in the music business; I felt like I belonged. By that I mean, I realized that up close and personal, these "stars" were still like me. More talented and successful, for sure – but they were doing the same things I did when I was on the street with everyday dopers and party goers.

They committed adultery(not all of them of course), and were sexually promiscuous, they drank alcohol, they did drugs, they lied, cursed, smoked, and did the same things my down and out friends did when I was living on the street. The difference was these rock stars had money and they had fame; they could do everything to the extreme and with style.

The irony didn't escape me. Backstage, away from the glitz and glitter - I learned that I had more in common with these "rock stars" than not. We were all doing the same things...

Yep, being around rock stars, albeit very talented and gifted individuals had a profound effect on how I viewed things. I began to realize that aside from the extraordinary musical gifts, most of these persons seemed to be very ordinary and weak – with weaknesses and problems like everybody else.

This revelation of the common thread of "sin" that was evident in all of us, in everyone from the hippies I knew and lived with, to the big time rock stars I was with; would be a truth that God was showing me though I wouldn't realize that until later. My eyes were slowly beginning to open.

Now only a few months after hitch-hiking to California; I'm flying to California on tour to play the Fillmore West where the FROST would be appearing with B.B. King. I was backstage every weekend at festivals and different venues meeting and partying with bands and artists whose songs were being played on the radio.

I was star struck for a while, simply because of the thrill of being so close to the singers and musicians I idolized. I was living a dream – at least for while anyway...

Meeting stars like B.B.King, Rod Stewart, Jeff Beck, Bog Segar, Ted Nugent, Three Dog Night; and many - many others (too many to list here) was very exciting. Unfortunately, I was constantly high on something so I was usually just standing around taking it all in – like a spectator at a sporting event. I was a casual observer – and much of what I heard and saw was not what you would want to share with your parents.

I suppose my short time of living on the street with nothing had made me look more closely at these rock stars, than I would have otherwise. Getting high with famous rock stars, and watching them up close, and living in that world of bright lights and adoring fans had a profound effect on me. I began to look past all the hype, the fancy stage clothes, and the incredible talent of these "stars" - and saw things I didn't like.

The bottom line was that my life on the street as a pauper, and now my life on the road with the rich and famous was teaching me lessons that you can't learn in a book – well – maybe the Bible; but I wasn't reading that book at that time in my life.

My Epiphany[b] !

I began to realize that whether rich or poor, unknown or famous, it didn't really matter. We all have the same problems and troubles to deal with, we all have our lust, anger, greed, and pride to struggle against. The shocking revelation that these rich and famous stars, with everything the world calls "success" - did the same things people on the streets with nothing did; was an epiphany to me!

I don't remember the moment, or the exact time when it hit me – when I realized I'm doing the same things I was doing when I was living on the road with nothing. I was discovering that I wasn't going to find happiness in this world of drugs, rock music, and fleeting pleasure.

To be honest, all I really knew at that time in my life was getting high, partying, and playing music. I was truly going nowhere, and in the back of my mind I knew it. I was trapped in a lifestyle that was fun and seductive in many ways; but was slowly destroying me – slowly leading me in circles.

I was on a merry – go – round, and like my life living in a dope house; there was no way for me to get off. Even if I had wanted to stop, or do something different with my life; I didn't know how – or where to turn for that to happen. I was lost and just following the hypnotizing beat of the world.

Little did I know that everything in my life was about to be shattered, and come crashing down; with me like Humpty Dumpty being scattered into a thousand pieces. I was about to enter a very dark and depressing world – a world that I was ill prepared to deal with.

I should make it clear at this juncture, many of the people in the secular rock and roll world were genuinely happy – really. But as I was finding out, it was only "momentary pleasure and happiness"... it wasn't lasting happiness. Not hardly.

---

b. epiphany: a moment of sudden revelation or insight. *bing search

The Big Show

On stage everything was staged, from the first strum of the guitar, to the spot light on the drummer's solo – it was all choreographed to please and entertain the audience. It was usually done in a professional manner as one would expect with a touring band on national prominence; but not everything.

By most standards, even back at that time; THE FROST were relatively tame. I mean <u>Alice Cooper</u> was tearing the heads off of chickens before going on stage, and one band I won't name would defecate on stage during their show.

That being said, the Frost did have a disgusting , sexually explicit segment to their show – right at the end. The band would close out the concert with the classic song from the English band, <u>The Animals</u>: / <u>We Got To Get Out Of This Place</u>.

The song would eventually go into a long drawn out guitar solo by Dick Wagner the band's lead singer. The music would gradually build into a loud and raucous crescendo – and then as the music reached a near climax(no pun intended); Dick Wagner would jump on his guitar – feigning sexual intercourse. * Please note – I've tried to say that as nicely as possible...

To be quite honest, based on the reactions of those in the audience I witnessed, and my own reaction; it wasn't all that impressive or entertaining. This was part of their "act", and why no one ever questioned it's effectiveness is still a mystery to me.

The "Facade"

According to Merriam Webster's dictionary, a facade is: *a false, superficial, or artificial appearance or effect . a way of behaving or appearing that gives other people a false idea of your true feelings or situation*

Okay, we all know that most movie sets in Westerns are fake, right? They have an old dusty dirty road, lined with store fronts and an old saloon, a bank and more.

Often those buildings, or so we think — are nothing more than one dimensional facades!

From the right camera angle, the buildings appear real, three dimensional; but as you enter the door you realize it's just a fake building — not real. It's all just a false front, to fool and deceive your eyes. That's what I learned working with the FROST. What the audiences saw for 90 minutes, was not what the band was really like when the lights went out on stage.

Without going into the actual words said(I can't remember the specific words now). I can tell you that the band members were not all one big happy family. The smiles and P.R. pictures you would see on the flyers/posters and album covers were not the reality that I saw when the band members were off stage.

I won't say they hated each other, but a love fest it wasn't. The best I can say without demeaning any of the members of the FROST specifically is this: They managed to put on their best face when on stage for the show, but when it was over; it was obvious the only thing that kept the band together was the "job or business" of being a professional band member.

Knowing that some of the band members(not everyone)really didn't like each other or get along that well when they weren't on stage performing; was disconcerting to say the least, and opened my eyes to the "bizz" side of being a secular musician. Hey you don't have to love each other, or even like each other to be a successful rock musician — just put on a great show!

In fairness to all of The Frost, they were professional when it came to practicing, and rehearsing for their shows... They never carried their personal dislike or attitudes towards one another on stage. I learned that it's possible to work with other people without everyone having to like each other.

The bottom line in the secular music industry as I came to realize, was "loving or liking" your band mates was not essential to be successful. Talent, and the ability to work with others trumped all else. Respect for each others musical gifts and prowess was a given; but no one was expected to "like or love" his or her fellow band mates.

It became apparent that being booked, busy and famous were rewards enough in and of themselves from what I could gather. The goal of being a rock star, or successful band/performer making decent money; and the sheer love of music meant being successful was everything. I had to find out later what God thinks true "success" is?

Sex, sex, sex...

Everyone knows that sex has always been linked to rock & roll, so I'm not going to do a walk down that road with you in this book. I will say however, that what may shock you on records or on stage pales in comparison to what goes on backstage and in the motel/hotel rooms when the concerts are over.

Groupies were something that I never quite fathomed, really. Why? Because they just seemed so naive and vulnerable, it was pathetic to see them so easily manipulated and used... They were always there at every concert, every town or city we would go to.

And sadly, they were easy prey for young guys in a famous band that happened to be appearing in their area. Anyone who has been involved with the secular rock music scene knows that it isn't just the music that musicians and bands love – sex and lots of it is right there in full display on and off stage. Sad but true.

The truth is, we were the guys moms and dads warned their daughters not to have anything to do with! Finding a beautiful young maiden to take back to the motel room at the end of the concert – was always our number one focus. Our lustful eyes were never satisfied.

One of the band members had a sexual appetite unlike anyone I've ever known in my life. While sex for most guys is pleasurable and can be a real problem in many ways whether married or not... This band member had an insatiable appetite for young ladies, and it was not uncommon for him to meet with several females in one evening.

I use the term "meet" loosely. All the stereotypes that moms and dads often associate with rock bands – like "loose sex, groupies, etc"; were played out before my eyes at every concert event we were involved with. Even for me, and I was no prude or saint; it was over the edge...

Without going into unnecessary detail, let me suffice to say I saw the lurid and perverse side of sex while touring as a Rd. Mgr. I was involved with unlawful sex to be sure, but what I saw and witnessed backstage made me realize that there are different levels of debauchery and depravity that a person can become involved with. The only question that really remained for me was: How far would I go down that path? I was a sinner and enjoyed sinning – hey, I'm just being honest. But now I was being confronted with opportunities to "push the envelope" a little further. I mean if can sin a little – why not try some things I thought I would never do. That "slippery slope" was right in front of me.

For some reason, my conscience would always remind me that I shouldn't go too far with a drug, or with sex... There was always a line in my mind that I would try to avoid crossing. You can do those drugs Michael, but don't do heroin – stay away from that. You can have a "one night stand" with one girl, but don't get involved with several girls, at least not in one evening. And, don't be involved with an orgy.

It's funny how we draw lines on what we will do and won't do when we are serving "sin"; but we do. The truth is eventually, if we continue in sin – we will end up doing things we thought we never would or could do. Sin is a cunning master, and we are most naive to think we can overcome it without divine intervention. I know – it was swallowing me whole.

13 Let no one say when he is tempted, "I am tempted by God"; for God cannot be tempted by evil, nor does He Himself tempt anyone. 14 But each one is tempted when he is drawn away by his own desires and enticed. 15 Then, when desire has conceived, it gives birth to sin; and sin, when it is full-grown, brings forth death. **James 1:13-15**

A HOUSE OF SAND

"But everyone who hears these sayings of Mine, and does not do them, will be like a foolish man who built his house on the sand. **Mt.7:26**

Life was good, very good for Jerry and me for a while. I mean we had jobs as roadies for one of the top bands in Michigan, and in the United States at the time. (1970-71) The FROST. We had toured both the East and West coasts, and had met and partied with some of the most famous rock stars in the world!

We had our own house, our own van, money/salary, and girls and friends who just wanted to be around a famous band. Drugs, groupies, parties – man o man – everyday was fun; hmm well at least most days...

Then things went South – really fast. The FROST, stopped getting bookings, and their short claim to fame(3 albums), and two tours, came to a crashing halt. We were told that the band was not doing well, and things were coming to a close for us. The band wouldn't be able to pay us a salary any longer.

To add to this dilemma, I got involved with distributing drugs on a small scale to low level dealers on the side, to make extra money. Big mistake! I had delivered some drugs to two small time dealers in Grand Blanc, Michigan; and one of them (or both of them), ripped me off for about 700.00 worth of drugs.

To this day I don't know if it was one, or both of them who stole the drugs from me – but I forgave them both. I know back then I might have done the same thing if I was in there situation.

The money they stole was money I owed to a local drug dealer(Danny) who had given me the drugs to sell for him. The only problem was, I didn't have his drugs or the money to pay him back. I knew Danny (who we partied with sometimes), was all business when it came to owing him money. I was scared – and realized I was in serious trouble.

All of a sudden, my entire life in a matter of a few weeks had come crashing down like a house of cards! I knew the guy I owed the money to, was all business – and he wasn't going to accept anything less than the money I owed him. Danny called me and gave me one week to have his money repaid - just one week.

I tried to come up with his money, but only managed to get $300.00 together for him. He wasn't going to accept that, and made it clear that business was business – and that if he didn't get his money a.s.a.p. - something very bad was going to happen.

He wasn't bluffing – it did!

From "Bad to Worse"

Have you ever heard the expression: IT CAN'T GET ANY WORSE! Well, what happened to me after that phone call with my dealer friend(Danny), the man I owed the money to can only be described as the "worst possible day in my life" - at least up to that point in my life. Looking back now, I know it could have been worse; but at that time in my life it ranked as the worst day of my life. (My bad days were starting to pile up...)

I remember I was smoking marijuana with a Hell's Angel[3] in a house across town, and having a sick premonition come over me that something very bad was happening across town at my home, where Jerry and I lived at the time.

It was about 2 am. in the morning and I told the people I was with, "I have to go," - "something bad is going on at my house." I left suddenly and went straight to my house.

When I arrived, I saw an old Buick idling in the driveway, and went to the front door and started to open it. Suddenly, a biker with a gun in his hand, put the gun to my head and tells me that we're being robbed. He tells me to shut up and get over against the wall.

I was a little crazy back then and I was screaming at him and very mad that he was in my home taking our musical equipment. Considering the circumstances, I was not acting very wisely by yelling and arguing with a man holding a loaded gun to my head.

The fact that I wasn't shot can only be attributed to the tender mercies of God in heaven, because I'm sure that I was close to dying - though in my drug induced state of mind I wasn't afraid - I was just very angry that we were being robbed.

At that time, Jerry and I were in a seven piece band, and the band members were all living with us. There were four bikers involved in this robbery and they were threatening to kill all of us; and they had all of the band members lined up against a wall in the dining room. My first reaction was anger, but it suddenly turned to fear when I saw the look of sheer terror on the faces of the members of our band.

By now I was starting to calm down, and realized the seriousness of the situation. Two band members had wet their pants because they were so frightened . I knew that this was "the bad thing" that was going to happen if I didn't pay back the money I owed for the drugs that were stolen from me. My worst fears about what might happen to me were happening; and I was powerless to do anything about it.

The entire robbery took less than an hour, and in that time the bikers had taken all of our amplifiers, all of our guitars, and a few other things that I can't recall. When it was all over our equipment was gone, and all of us were visibly shaken by what had just happened. We were literally all in a state of shock.

The good news was, we were all alive – and no one was hurt. The bad news – the bikers/The Outlaws – had told all of us that if we went to the authorities they would come after us one by one and execute each of us. A vote was take and we decided 4 to 3 not to go to the police.

I wanted to inform the police about what had happened, but knew I could never live with my self if anyone was killed because of that decision. This was the day everything really began to fall apart at the seams.

That was the day that everything unraveled in my life. The band fell apart and most of the members moved out that day. Our landlord wanted his monthly rent, and we were broke and couldn't pay him. He evicted us, and we were only days away from being out on the street. Life as I knew it was over, and in just a few days I was going to be homeless once again.

Funny how life has away of repeating itself sometimes. Only thing was – it wasn't funny. I couldn't believe it! Here I am once again homeless, and penniless... Does the story of the prodigal son come to mind? Only I had never really left God – I had never found Him in the first place.

A Dark Hole Of Despair

I remember it was in the Fall, and I was once again on the street with nothing – no money, no car, no possessions really to speak of, and no where to go. I was really discouraged, and now the thought of being homeless and living on the street terrified me. I didn't know where to go – and I just walked the street in despair – cold and very afraid. That was a horrible day – a really rotten day that I'll never forget.

I remember going to a close friend Tommy I had known for years, thinking I'm sure he'll let me stay with him – at least for the night or a few days. When I went to the front door, my friend came to the door and greeted me. I'm thinking okay, he's going to help me; I'll get to come out of the cold and be safe and warm.

Wrong!

Tommy told me he couldn't let me stay that night because he had a girl spending the night with him. I told him I would sleep in the breezeway, the small hall that was there just before you enter the main section of the home. Sorry bro, I can't let you stay here tonight.

To say I was hurt would be understating my feelings of betrayal and anger at being turned away by a dear friend on a cold night in the middle of Autumn. As I turned away tears filled my eyes; I was crying and mumbling as I slowly walked down the street towards nowhere in particular...

I probably could have went to a shelter(though I didn't know where any were), and I could have went to the Salvation Army and they would have probably given me temporary assistance; but for some reason that never dawned on me as a way out of my predicament.

To make matters worse, I had burned my hand very severely making "marijuana tea" in our kitchen while leaning against a stove. I hate to admit it but I was so wrecked/stoned – that I couldn't feel my hand being burnt by the electric stove until it was too late. My head was so dulled by being high that I was slow to react to my flesh being literally cooked!

That was the sure sign that my world of bliss and comfort was coming to a crashing end... Instead of going to the emergency room(no one was in any condition to drive me there anyways), I just put some ointment on my hand and suffered through the pain. I walked around in that condition for the next 3-4 weeks.

I thought I'll call my brother who lives in Flint, and ask him if I can stay with him – at least for a while until I can find some place to stay. After calling my brother, he was nice enough to agree to let me come and stay with him for at least a while.

I was happy for the moment that I had found a place to go to, especially with winter just around the corner. My happiness was to be short-lived as I was about to soon discover. Upon my arrival to my brother's small apartment on the East side of Flint, I learned this was not going to be a picnic or walk in the park for either of us.

My brother was himself at that time in a very deep depression, and when I moved in I realized that both of us were emotionally down and in no condition to help each other. For the first time in my life I had sunk down into a really dark abyss of despair and fear; and other negative emotions such as loneliness, and hopelessness.

I had never really experienced any of these dark emotions before, so I was overwhelmed at having these feelings and very confused about everything. I was in a dark hole of depression and despair; and saw no way out. My brother was of no help to me at the time – he was battling his own demons of depression. We were like the "blind leading the blind" - a most pitiful state of affairs to be sure.

It Gets Darker and Darker

Just when I thought it couldn't get any worse – it got worse! I began to have suicidal thoughts, something I had never had in my life; in fact I had never been depressed for more than a few days, I had always had a very positive attitude even under the most trying of circumstances. Depression, real deep penetrating depression like I was experiencing was something I had never experienced.

But now, somehow I felt overwhelmed by the darkness that surrounded me. I had thoughts of taking my own life, thoughts of homosexuality entered my mind that I had never had before; and I was sensing fear and other powerful negative emotions that were causing me to feel paralyzed and spiritually drained through my entire being.

It was at this time, that I began to cry out to God, if there is a God to help me. I was desperate, really feeling hopeless but was not going down without a fight. I cried out to God in my soul, and in my spirit to reveal Himself to me. I began to read the book: The Imitation of Christ, by Thomas Kempis and other religious books, seeking answers and help for my horrible feelings of utter despair and hopelessness.At this time I didn't know anything about spiritual warfare, demons, or what the Bible had to say about being oppressed or tempted and attacked by Satan. It wouldn't be until many years later that I would learn that Satan was trying to destroy me and take me to hell. I was ignorant of his devices and schemes, but God is His mercy was allowing me to break out of this pit of darkness and despair.

It wasn't long after this period of deep depression that I was in – that I managed to move out and into an apartment of my own. I was still climbing out of my personal depression, and slowly getting back to thinking clearly and positively like I always had in the past; but I still had a lingering sense that there was a battle going on all around me. I didn't know that the battle I was sensing was the battle for my soul, the battle that every soul since the time of Adam has had to face – even Jesus himself.

This was around the time that I really began my quest for spiritual meaning for my life. I wasn't sure if it was in the Bible, I hadn't discounted that, but I was open to exploring everything in my hopes of finding peace, and rest for my soul. This was point of fact – the lowest point in my life up to that time.

I was convinced that drugs, sex, and rock – and -roll, were not going to give me the answers I needed – that I was desperate to find. At this point in my life, I could have been swayed by any number of religious views or teachings; because I was wanting to find answers for my life. Where is God? Is He real? Why am I here? Why is there so much evil all around me?

It wasn't long after my battle with depression, while I was searching for something to give me answers to these questions, that I was introduced to Scientology. That would prove to be another dead end street; but it would take me over a year to learn the truth about this seductive religious cult that had drawn me into it's intricate web of deceit.

Let me say at this point, I do not believe "all paths lead to God" as some teach. I do believe all religions and religious philosophies have some truth or at least a measure of truth that is mixed in with a good measure or degree of deception and lies -when held up to the light of the Bible.

I've learned after years of studying the major world religions, and numerous religious philosophies (which Scientology is); that only the Bible/the holy scriptures and the teachings of Jesus Christ are worthy of being considered "truth." To be even more clear, I believe it is actually only the person of Jesus Christ that can be summarily referred to as: The Truth.

Jesus, Himself declared this startling statement:

> *Jesus said to him, "I am the way, the truth, and the life. No one comes to the Father except through Me.* **JN.14:6**

It was astounding to the religious leaders at that time to hear such a provocative and mind boggling statement from this young Nazarene who had shaken up the status quo of his day. Not surprisingly, that statement – that Jesus spoke – declaring Himself to be the "truth – the only way to the Father" is still ruffling religious feathers today. He leaves it to us to either believe Him, or not.

I choose to believe.

MY INTRODUCTION TO SCIENTOLOGY

This part of my story is about my experiences while I was into Scientology; and not just as a client or student of it's religious philosophy – but as a contractual member of staff in Detroit, Michigan.

The facts presented here are as best as I can recall them after many years being away from Scientology, and some of the names of those I worked with on staff in Detroit have been changed . I assert that what I'm about to tell you is the truth, and is my personal testimony of what happened to me during my short time as a paid staff member in the Scientology Organization during the period approximately from 1971 -1972.

I don't remember the exact months when I arrived and began my role as a paid member on staff in Detroit, or the exact month when I left. What I do remember though is that my contract was not legally binding because at the time I signed it; I was only 19 or 20 and you had to be 21 for any contract in Michigan to be considered legally binding. I forged my father's signature without his knowledge in order to join staff.

That fact will become very significant later on in this story, when I talk about my escape and departure from Scientology.

I pray you or anyone contemplating joining Scientology, or any religious cult or group will read my testimony of how God brought me out of this seductive snare of Satan – and avoid being drawn into their webs of deceit and deception.

As I said earlier, joining a religious cult is far easier than it is to exit one! Like the unsuspecting mouse who enters the trap door that only swings one way – to his certain death; is the poor soul who joins a group or cult whose paths lead straight to hell.

It was all too easy for me and others to enlist in Scientology and become disciples and students of this bizarre, yet alluring religious organization. But trying to leave, trying to walk away from it now that's another matter.

Here is my story of my escape from Scientology, and how God delivered me completely and wonderfully - much to the the disdain and angst of those I worked with on staff in Detroit – and of course, the Devil himself.

My First Meeting

I can't remember who it was that invited me to my first meeting where I would hear a lecture/presentation on what Scientology was about; but I do remember that meeting. It was in a nice office building somewhere near downtown Flint, in Michigan. I went to my first meeting skeptical and cynical to be sure; but inwardly hoping that maybe – just maybe this might be something to help me out of my dark days of depression.

The staff there were friendly and professional, and I didn't sense they were out to run a scam on me, or take advantage of me. I listened intently as they told me about L. Ron Hubbard's Best Selling book: <u>DIANETICS THE MODERN SCIENCE OF MENTAL HEALTH</u>[2]; and how it was changing the world by the truths contained in it. I wasn't buying it – but I was listening.

I didn't sign up that day, but I left thinking it was very interesting and worth looking into further. Very shortly after that first meeting I decided to sign up for a short course that was only for about 6 weeks as I recall. Those meetings were enough to convince me that there was something to this Scientology that seemed to be helping me in some small ways.

Stand Up!

At one of my first meetings after signing up for a short course in Scientology I began to find out how strange some of their exercises were – very strange indeed! We would pair off with another person who had signed up for the training, and begin doing exercises with each other.

One such exercise was designed to improve one's "intention", or to put it another way – one's ability to focus all your mental energy on one thing, on one object. We would stare at an object, say an ashtray – and then with every bit of concentration begin to shout at the ashtray to: STAND UP!

That would be repeated over and over again, until your partner, and the staff member there with Scientology felt your "intention" was satisfactory. It was comforting to look around the room and see other adults like myself - staring at ashtrays and shouting at the top of their lungs:

Stand up! Stand up! (this would be repeated over and over)

Now, before you scoff or laugh at "how could anyone do such a silly thing?" please understand that as ridiculous as it may sound. In some strange way – it actually had a positive effect on me and those there in attendance. Perhaps a psychologist can explain why that is, but at the time it was very stimulating.

Of course, all of this may remind some of you of Yoko Ono's famous "screaming song" that many deem "art". Looking back, it's hard to believe I wasn't more averse to the idea of yelling at an ashtray – but then again everyone around me was doing the same thing. Somehow you don't feel as foolish when everyone around you is acting foolish with you!

Eye To Eye

Another unusual exercise that we all engaged in was designed to help you confront others. The idea behind this bizarre exercise was to teach an individual how to better confront other persons, and "things" in one's life.

To accomplish this, we the students were told to sit in chairs, facing each other at a distance of about four feet – with our eyes looking directly into the other person's eyes. Now, that sounds fairly easy, but the rules were: You couldn't blink and you couldn't look away.

If you blinked or looked away, you had to start over and the entire exercise would be timed. I don't remember how long I managed to go without blinking or looking away, but I eventually succeeded in doing the exercise correctly to the satisfaction of the Scientologist who was monitoring us.

I remember my eyes burning, watering, and having extreme difficulty doing this particular activity. The really strange thing is that it was very challenging and exhilarating to actually succeed in doing this otherwise silly exercise. Looking into another person's eyes without blinking and without looking away for fifteen or so minutes in some strange way made me feel like I had accomplished something.

There were other training exercises along those lines, and several lectures about the teachings and beliefs of Scientology. I didn't understand what I was walking into – what I was about to become entangled in, but I was slowly thinking that maybe Scientology was something that could help me.

I started to believe that I had found something that was worth giving myself to – something that might give my life meaning and purpose.

I don't remember most of what was being taught at those meetings, but I do remember that the meetings were well organized, and they had an enormous amount of literature, and things to support their teachings and philosophy. I wasn't convinced that Scientology was legitimate, or something I wanted to commit to or be deeply involved with – but I was slowly being drawn into it week by week.

In a very short time, I had become entangled in it's enticing web of deceit and deception. Scientology's promise of making a person "happy and free" -for all who followed it's teachings and axioms was something I longed for with all my being.

I was very close to making a heartfelt decision to go all out, and become a full time member on staff as a Scientologist. This would prove to be one of the single worst decisions of my entire life. (the list was growing...)

My "Five Year Contract"

It was only a few weeks after my first meetings in Flint, Michigan that I decided to commit myself fully to Scientology by signing a contract to join staff in Detroit. Part of my reason for this was purely financial; I figured by being on staff I would receive training, classes, and auditing(I'll explain this later); without having to pay for them.

Little did I know how my life was about to become entangled in a web of intense "brainwashing" and indoctrination that would find me soon looking for a way out of Scientology; something that proved to be extremely difficult for me to do.

At that time, living in Michigan to sign a contract that was legally binding, you had to be twenty one – and I was only 19. I knew my father wouldn't sign for me, and I didn't want to ask him anyways with our relationship being estranged at the time. So I decided that I would simply forge my father's signature, and hope that they didn't bother to check with my father about that.

I remember going over the contract options with a Scientology staff member, and having them explain the terms of the contracts they were offering at that time. The shortest contract available was a 5 year contract, and then they went from 10, to 20, 25, 50, 100 years - and even "perpetual" or never ending contracts as I remember. (*see note at chapter's end)

I figured a 5 year contract wasn't too scary, and if I decided to leave it would be easier with a short term contract. Besides, my backup plan, my out – was the fact that I had forged my father's signature on the contract. This turned out later to be something that protected me when I finally left Scientology over a year later.

The Detroit Organization

After signing a five year contract, I moved what few belongings I had at the time, and moved in with several other staff members in what can only be described as a "commune". We were all Scientologists on staff, under contract and very young; with everyone under the age of twenty five years of age.

The contract wasn't very detailed, at least not the five year contract I signed; but it did make it clear that I was legally bound to work for Scientology for the next five years of my life. Many other staff members had signed contracts much more lengthy than me; and some had even decided to make life long careers as full time staff members with

Scientology.

At first, I was very excited – like the feeling a person gets when they are on a trip to a new place they've never been to before. The first few weeks I was too busy getting familiar with everything at the "org" in Detroit as we called the building where we conducted our work, to really think about much of anything else. I won't say I was having fun, but it was certainly an interesting time for me during those first few weeks.

When I say "busy", I mean busy as in working from the early morning starting at 8 am., until late in the evening; most days until 10 or 11 pm. There was little time for relaxation or leisure, because we were required to be either studying and involved with training exercises, or doing an assigned task that each of us had at the org.

Poor & Hungry

The reason so many of us had to live together in one place, in one large house was simple: We had to or we couldn't survive! I can't remember the exact amount of pay that we were paid at that time(it was in the early 70's), but I do remember it was about 15-20 dollars a week total.

That meager amount of money was for one week's work, which was on average about 100 hours of work at the org. Even back then, that wasn't enough for a person on their own to live on let alone own a car or to buy groceries.

By living together in one large home, we all managed to buy enough basic staples, eggs, milk, bread, potatoes, etc; to get by. I was used to not having money, and being hungry wasn't anything new to me from my time hitch-hiking around the country. Still, I was surprised at how little we were being paid, and how much work all of us were doing as staff members.

Some of the staff members were from wealthy families, and didn't have to live in the "commune" style housing that the majority of us were living in at the time. They obviously had a different perspective than we did for obvious reasons. It didn't take me long to realize that I wasn't going to get rich being on staff in Detroit as a Scientologist.

Most of us didn't have our own transportation, so driving together everyday in a car pool was the norm. Our lives were very regimented and disciplined, if for no other reason we spent almost every waking hour together with little privacy or time away from other staff members. The only time I really could be alone to think without distractions was I went to the bathroom or when I was in bed sleeping.

My job for most of the day at the org, was to oversee the "Mail Department", and organize and send out daily Scientology promotional materials to several states here in the Midwest. This meant being responsible for addressing and mailing out each day – twenty to thirty thousand pieces of mail. This task consumed most of my time, and also ensured that I was dead tired at the end of each workday.

Everyone, regardless of what their title or job was in the org was required to look very professional and neat in appearance. All of the guys wore dress slacks and white shirts and ties, and the ladies all wore a similar look with dark blue skirts and crisp white blouses. We may have been poor and hungry, but outwardly we looked very sharp.

We were trained to be courteous and friendly, and to treat all our clients - really "paying customers" professionally. We were always on our best behavior when a new person or regular client was in our presence; which is not unlike other businesses where the atmosphere quickly changes the moment anyone from the "outside" enters the business. (more on this later)

L. Ron Hubbard / The founder

HAIL RON!

82

Upon arriving at the org in the morning at 8 am., we would all assemble in a larger room in the upper level of the building for what seemed to be a "pep rally" of sorts. The Executive Director (Suzy), a small fiery lady with clear blue eyes and a penetrating gaze would lead us all in our morning cheer to Ron.

A picture of L. R. Hubbard[5], who was the founder and man who established and created Scientology, hung on the wall and we would all stand and face his portrait. Then our Director,Suzy would lead us in a loud and boisterous cheer to Ron as she liked to call him. She would say things like: "We're going to save the world" - We're going to create a new world!"

Soon the room would be filled with shouts and cheers, "Hail Ron! - Hail Ron!" I admit it seemed a little bizarre and strange to be staring at a picture of a man I knew little about, and even stranger shouting praises to this image on the wall; but I did. Everyone else did too. I'm certain I wasn't the only one thinking that this was over the top – but, no one said anything.

After this short meeting, which usually only lasted about 5 minutes; our dynamic leader would clap her hands together loudly – and exclaim loudly, "Let's go save the world" - or words to that effect. Everyday was like that – a staff meeting where we "hailed Ron" and then scrambled off to our assigned duties.

If you're reading this now, and thinking you had to know this was a religious cult, or at the very least something very strange and weird – you would be right. It didn't take me long to see "red flags" going up all over the place in my mind. I was beginning to have 2nd thoughts about my involvement with Scientology even in the first few months I was there – but in my case, I really had no place to go to. That made things a little more complicated.

Life In The Detroit Org...

I had no social life really, actually none of us did - we were just too busy being busy at the org each day to do anything other than work, sleep, and start all over again the next day. One day faded into the next day until my life became one big blur of activity; basically doing the same things over and over again and again. Always being busy and tired was our "normal."

Besides our specific duties and responsibilities which all of us had to do each day, we were also required to spend a certain amount of time being trained and studying the teachings and tenets of Scientology. New teachings and lessons would be constantly released to us on staff, and we were required to spend time learning and reading the materials and lessons that were given to us.

My diet was meager at best, with snacks and junk food a constant source of quick energy along with coffee and pop to keep me going. After months of working long hours day in and day out, and living on a very poor diet with little nutritional content I was beginning to feel weak and drained physically and mentally.

At that time I began to seriously question my involvement with Scientology. I was having serious doubts about all of it, but I still held out hope that maybe Scientology could help me – maybe it was still what I had

been looking for. I wasn't ready to leave, or try to leave; but the thought of getting out of Scientology was beginning to cross my mind.

Oh – and as far as our pay or compensation went; it was not enough for anyone to live on without outside financial help from some other source. We were working on average 90 to 120 hours a week, and I don't remember the exact amount we were paid; but I do remember my average pay was about $20.00 per week.

That was well below minimum wage at that time, and the least amount of money I had ever been paid for jobs I had done in the past... it was by anyone's standards – abysmally low.

If those of us on staff were not living together in one house, and pooling our money together none of us would have survived.

We did the best to buy the basics such as milk, potatoes,cereal and eggs (which was our typical daily diet), but to be sure we were living on far less than most people were having everyday. That fact rubbed me the wrong way and after time, I began to resent the long hours and ridiculously small pay we all were getting. I was not alone in feeling that way I'm sure.

Now that I've shared how I first became involved with Scientology, and what my first impressions and feelings were towards it; I think a brief explanation of what Scientology is, and what it's beliefs and teachings are is in order.

DIANETICS/The Book Of Lies

Most of what we were taught and had to learn while we were on staff as Scientologists in Detroit , was based on the book: Dianetics The Modern Science Of Mental Health[4], that L.R. Hubbard wrote. Keep in mind that what the Bible is to Christians, the book - Dianetics is to Scientologists.

So before I explain more fully just what Scientology is and what it's teachings and doctrines are; it's necessary to first look at this "book" which most of Scientology is built upon.

Much of what I share here is taken directly or indirectly from the book, DIANETICS..., and also from Wikipedia, as well as my own personal experience as a practitioner and member on staff at the Scientology Organization in Detroit in the early 70's. Any other sources are listed as well, and may be found at the end of each chapter of this book.

Scientology was founded and established by the late L. Ron Hubbard[3], a world famous science fiction writer – whose books are well read and known world over. His books can be found in most Bookstores throughout the world, and he is also revered by many as a noted lecturer, thinker, and philosopher of sorts.

Scientology, was founded in 1952, and in 1953 L. Ron Hubbard established the "Church of Scientology", which was based upon the tenets and principles put forth in his book: DIANETICS.

In May of 1950, Hubbard's book: **Dianetics**: <u>The Modern Science of Mental Health</u>, was published. His book entered the New York Times best-seller list on June 18th, and stayed there until December 24th of that year.

Dianetics, is the book that Scientology is based upon, and a book that has caused no small controversy since it's publication. Two of Hubbard's key supporters at the time were John W. Campbell, the editor of Astounding Science Fiction, and Dr. Joseph A. Winter.

Winter had hoped Scientology would be accepted by the medical community, and submitted papers outlining the principles and teachings of Scientology to the Journal of the American Medical Association, and the American Journal of Psychiatry in 1949. His efforts were fruitless, they were soundly rejected.

Dianetics Explained

The following definition is taken from Wikepedia ... http://en.wikipedia.org/ where Dianetics is defined: (http://en.wikipedia.org/wiki/Scientology), and how it is applied as a form of treatment for human beings suffering from a wide range of mental, emotional, physical, and spiritual problems.

It is a very brief summation and not meant to explain every facet of how Dianetics is carried out within the structure of Scientology. It is simply a snapshot of how Dianetics can be viewed to the casual observer.

Dianetics uses a counseling technique known as *auditing*, to enable conscious recall of traumatic events in an individual's past. It was originally intended to be a new <u>psychotherapy</u> and was not expected to become the foundation for a new religion. Hubbard variously defined Dianetics as a spiritual healing technology and an organized science of thought. The stated intent of Dianetics is to free individuals of the influence of past traumas by systematic exposure and removal of the *engrams* these events have left behind, in a process called *clearing*.

My Own Perspective

As a new initiate of Scientology, you were expected to purchase and study the book, DIANETICS ; and to know it well. After all, as I soon discovered most of what Scientologists taught and practiced could be traced back to that book and the lectures which were based on the book's contents.

I spent a lot of time learning the basic tenets of Hubbard's philosophy as outlined in his book; and eventually became so familiar with it that I was able to quote verbatim many of the key teachings found in it. That was how many of us spent out free time; studying and memorizing it.

In fact, I later went on to teach and present the basic ideas contained in the Dianetics book to visitors to the Org who wanted to know what Scientology was all about. New people interested in Scientology, were given a brief presentation and then someone on staff would try to sign them up...

What I'm going to tell you has probably changed since the time I was with Scientology, and is probably much slicker and polished as anything would be as it is improved upon over a period of time. From what I've read and researched, these ideas are still essentially the same as what we were presenting to the public when I was still on staff.

As you read the philosophy and ideas that are the foundation for Scientology please keep in mind that the author and creator of this worldwide religious philosophy – was a renown science fiction writer himself. That fact may help you appreciate the unusual explanation Mr. Hubbard presents as the basis for both his book "Dianetics ..."; as well as everything else taught within the realm of the Church of Scientology.

A Big Game

Millions of years ago, human beings or "thetans" as Mr. Hubbard likes to refer to us as; were bored and came up with the idea of creating the earth and using it to play with – as a kind of game to have fun with. There was one big problem.

The concept of M.E.S.T., an acronym for: Matter, Energy, Space, and Time is used to describe the world we call "reality" - or the world we all know and live in down here on earth. We created these bodies to have fun, to do something entertaining and challenging; hence the idea of a "big game" that we all devised for our amusement. Please don't start laughing just yet... The problem was the unforeseen consequence of "accidents" and mishaps happening to us – to our bodies – to our emotions.

These unfortunate events in our lives, caused us pain and terrible memories that adversely affected us in many ways. The painful memories of tragic events and accidents are called "engrams". Over time these bad memories cause us to be unhappy, maladjusted, and generally a mess as human beings. Scientology offers a way to eliminate these "engrams."

Scientology teaches that the mind is divided into two parts: The "analytical mind", which is a rational mechanism where consciousness takes place. And the "reactive mind", where all painful and emotionally traumatic and charged memories are stored.

Mr. Hubbard poses the belief that engrams, or painful memories over time cripple and harm the individual and ultimately result in unhappy and under achieving human beings – or thetans as he prefers to call us. In time, if left unchecked a person will lose his or her true identity.

According to DIANETICS, and Mr. Hubbard's teachings as I was taught – the way to eliminate these painful memories is through a process called "auditing". In auditing, a trained "auditor" will use an "E-meter" to guide an individual back to these painful memories, and use select questions to erase these "engrams" forever.

You might compare these sessions to a person seeing a therapist, psychiatrist or priest for counseling or confession. There are similarities, and differences of course, but it is in fact intended to help individuals deal with spiritual, emotional, mental, and even physical problems of every possible kind.

The End Game

Oh, and one more thing – auditing wasn't cheap! No sir, that's one thing I remember clearly. If you wanted help, it wasn't going to be free, it wasn't for everyone – not really. Yes, we talked about saving the world, helping people get free; but in reality – we all knew that if you were poor – you were probably destined to remain stuck where you were, wherever that might be. The bottom line was – Scientology at it's heart was a business.

The goal as we were taught, was to go "clear", which simply meant that a person had received enough auditing to be free from the terrible engrams that all of us have within us. This of course doesn't happen overnight, in truth it takes thousands of dollars generally speaking, and hundreds of hours of auditing sessions for that to happen.

That goal in Scientology was rolled into a slogan that is known as: "Let's Clear The Planet". To be sure, "going clear" was what all of us talked about, what we dreamed about; and what only a few of us were able to do. Why? Going clear was extremely expensive to achieve, and even as staff members it was not something that we could afford to do.

As staff members, we were entitled to some free auditing each week. I can't remember now how many hours we were afforded each week, but it wasn't much; and it was clear(no pun intended), that going clear would take a long, long time if one's only means of getting there was as a staff member. I realized very quickly that my path to going clear, would take years if I was only going to have a few hours of auditing each week.

Please understand, that going "clear" was no small deal, it was a very big deal, the first major goal for every Scientologist; whether you were on staff or just an ordinary Scientologist. There were more levels that one could climb or reach after that; but this was the first big prize that everyone in Scientology wanted.

Before I discuss where a person could go after "going clear", let me first describe how things looked to me from someone on the inside of Scientology's web of deceit.

Money, Money, Money

I was only able to receive a few hours of auditing myself each week because that's all I could afford, and those few hours were benefits that were given to all staff members based on the number of hours you worked each week. I don't remember the exact formula for that, but it wasn't anything to write home about.

What I did notice however that was those clients who had money, who were wealthy and able to pay for the many hours of auditing necessary to go up the different levels on one's way to "clear" - did so with amazing speed! Yes indeed, if you had money, and some of our regular customers did; you were destined to go clear in a relatively short amount of time.

The lessons learned were clear(there I go again), if a person had money he could become free, clear as we called it – and even go on further than that to even higher and higher levels of inner awareness and consciousness. The only thing was, it wasn't cheap! It was obvious that Scientology catered to those who had money, and if you didn't – well let's just say your road to being "free and clear" - hmm, was going to be a slow road to hoe.

I know that some of our clients or customers as I really came to view them, were able to go through the entire process in only a relatively short period of time. The reason for that was they had money. From my lowly position as a regular member of staff making a mere pittance every week; the prospect of ever getting any serious auditing or help from Scientology (even if it were possible, which I had serious doubts about), would take years to experience.

I soon began to conclude that any hope I had of being helped myself through auditing, was not likely to happen anytime soon. At this juncture, you may be wondering why I would give an serious thought to the idea of paying for auditing – surely you must have seen it to be a complete hoax – a sham! You would be wrong.

The Testimonies...

As strange as it may sound, I actually saw a significant number of individuals helped by the "auditing sessions"; and some of them were quite dramatic. It was hearing these "testimonies" from different individuals claiming that they had been healed or had experienced wonderful changes in their lives that beguiled and bewitched me.

There was one woman who was a doctor, who had tried all of the possible traditional means of traditional medicine to alleviate her physical condition – all to no avail. One day she came walking out of one of her many auditing sessions shouting loudly, "I'm healed, I'm healed" - "I can walk without any pain".

I don't believe she was acting or being told to do that, nor do I believe she was imagining the whole thing in her mind apart from reality. What I do believe is that, she believed she was healed – and she was! Belief – is a powerful thing, and she believed that whatever happened that day in her auditing session worked, and for her that day – it did!

While there weren't a large number of testimonies or reports of that kind on any regular basis; there were enough of them to make me think that Scientology – strange as it may be, just might be legitimate after all. I had my doubts at that time about whether I should remain in Scientology or not; but had yet to reach a final verdict one way or the other about that.

Years later, after I became a Christian and began to understand the Bible; and realized that Satan can do signs and wonders, and can feign miracles if the end game is to deceive and entrap people into believing lies... The same demons that can afflict a person or torment them; can withdraw that sickness or stop tormenting them; if it means leading them into the depths of greater spiritual darkness.

One more point on these "testimonies", which gave me pause before I could make a judgment one way or the other as to the efficacy and truth about "auditing" - and Scientology in general.

It wasn't until years later, after studying the Bible extensively, and reading books on cults and other world religions; that I realized that all religions and cults have some "truth" in their teachings – in their doctrines.

This is how Satan has deceived so many souls through the ages, with "religion"! He will mix just enough truth in with his lies and deceitful doctrines to beguile and ensnare unsuspecting individuals who are ignorant of his devices. Scientology is just one of many paths to hell, but like so many other false religions and philosophies – it has some things that people find attractive and appealing .

Going O.T.

Going clear, which at that time would take approximately six to eight months if you had enough money to pay for the hundreds of hours necessary to do that – was not the "end game". It was a notable achievement, if you can call it that; but it wasn't the final destination for dedicated Scientologists – that was much further down the road to spiritual enlightenment. That lofty place in Scientology is known as being: O.T. (Operating Thetan)

An individual who has reached this level in Scientology has to go through several additional phases of training and auditing, to finally reach the place where they can "operate from without their physical bodies" - or so I was told. I never reached the level of "clear", let alone the high status and state of being, O.T. - so I am relating to you the reader what I was told at the time

I was in Scientology at that time. (1970-71)

You should know that persons who had reached this pinnacle within the world of Scientology were given "Rock Star" status! I should know about that, because I lived with them and hung out with them only a year or so before becoming a member of Scientology. Jealousy, envy and pride were not uncommon emotions felt by many of us who were stuck on the bottom of the spiritual hierarchy that we all were a part of. Like it or not, we knew that these O.T.'s as we called them were where we all wanted to be. Getting there was another thing altogether.

Go Sell A Book!

As with any business or organization, you have slow days. Well, one day there was nothing going on, no new visitors, nothing at all – the place was dead. Our zesty and restless Director would have none of that.

She came marching into the main room up in the front of the building where the entrance was; and handed those of us standing there all a book. The book was of course, L. R. Hubbard's flagship book/DIANETICS... Suzy literally pushed us all out the front door and told us, " go sell some books! You have one hour, don't come back until you've sold all the books!" Walking up and down Livernois Ave. in Detroit on a sunny day, with 3 paperback books of Dianetics in my hands; I began to confront strangers with my pitch to buy one of our books.

I didn't sell any books that afternoon, and I had to force myself to sound sincere and excited about selling books to strangers on the street. It was around this time that my net experience of being on staff as a Scientologist in Detroit was taking a serious toll on my emotions and psyche.

Being on staff full time was hard work, and the long hours and meager diet, along with the monotony and sameness that was our daily routine had worn me out. I was kept so busy doing tasks within the org everyday(they wouldn't let you be idle while you were inside the org), that there was little time to be alone, or to simply relax.

I didn't realize it at the time, but the nonstop busyness, the constant studying, and lack of privacy – along with a poor nutritional diet; are all tactics used by cults to "brainwash" individuals into compliance. I wasn't savvy enough to know what was happening to me – but I knew I didn't like how I felt, and the robotic routine was definitely taking a toll on me.

I was having 2nd thoughts about my involvement with Scientology – no, make that 3rd and 4th thoughts; and began to have a sick inward feeling – I'm trapped! With no one to talk to about my doubts and misgivings; I just sank deeper and deeper into a kind of unemotional – mechanical way of carrying on...

To be honest, I think many of us on staff were just going through our daily routines with out much emotion or passion; at least that's how everyone appeared to act. If anyone was having negative thoughts about Scientology, or feeling badly about anything they were experiencing – they were keeping it to themselves.

Besides, we were usually surrounded by several staff members which made it difficult to share anything with anyone without fear of being reported to our superior, who seemed to pop in at any given moment.

Without exaggerating, I can say that the atmosphere in that org was anything but relaxing or free; hardly – in reality it was endless hours of work with little or no time for talking, and certainly not if it was a complaint or criticism of Scientology. That was just understood by all of us.

To openly criticize or complain about anything going on around you was simply something we all knew was not acceptable behavior for staff members. I never heard anyone openly voice a complaint or criticism during my entire time as a Scientologist in Detroit.

In spite of all the confusion, and weirdness surrounding the inward activities and behavior of staff members; there was a sense that we were all involved in something new, different – and exciting. It was that aspect of being involved with Scientology that appealed to many of us on staff; at least that was how I was reading others at the time...

This state of being conflicted and mentally and emotionally torn; was draining on me – and I began to realize I was in over my head in more ways than I could have every imagined!

BLINDED BY SATAN

But even if our gospel is veiled, it is veiled to those who are perishing, whose minds the god of this age has blinded, who do not believe, lest the light of the gospel of the glory of Christ, who is the image of God, should shine on them. **2 CO. 4:3-4**

They say "Hindsight is 20/20." Years later, after I had left Scientology; I would ask myself, "How could I have been so gullible, so dumb to fall for such a scam as Scientology?" Yes, things always look clearer once were away from the fog and the shadows that we as human beings often find ourselves trapped in.

There are a myriad of paths that lead to hell, some so obvious that Ray Charles could see them with his sunglasses on. But sadly, there are many roads to the abyss that are not so easily discerned, even by learned and sophisticated sojourners here in the earth.

On the other hand, we all know that it only takes a "drop of poison" mixed in with the whole, to kill someone. This is true of course with religion, as I've discovered that all religions, even the most primitive and unstructured have some element of truth within them.

So even though I was disturbed and taken back by much of what I was seeing and experiencing as an insider, there were just enough things to impress me and cause me to not completely dismiss or discount

Scientology outright... At the time I was confused, perplexed, and questioning everything and anything. I was searching – but to be honest at that time of my life – I wasn't even sure what that was.

One thing was for certain, I had serious doubts about my involvement with Scientology and was very skeptical and cynical about this philosophy that I had only a few months earlier embraced with open arms.

I don't believe all religions lead to God, or that all religions are equal or that they are all paths to enlightenment. On the contrary, just for the record; I have come to believe that only through a personal relationship with Jesus Christ can a person truly know God, and have eternal life.

Of course, at the time I was on staff in Detroit living as a Scientologist that was the furthest thing from my mind. I was blinded to the truth that the above scriptures so plainly declare. It would be at least another year before my eyes would be opened clearly to the truth found in the gospel – in the teachings within the Holy Bible.

It wasn't any one thing that caused me to question my involvement in Scientology at that time. It was an accumulation of many different things I had experienced, that I had seen and heard that eventually weighed heavy on my heart.

Living almost every waking hour with other Scientologists on staff; you get to know them better than you know your own family members – really! I heard and saw things that gave me serious pause about the integrity and validity of Scientology as the "way to save the world", as we were often quick to blurt out to one another.

Something Ain't Right!

Like a bad odor in a room, but you can't quite discern exactly where it's coming from, or an out of tune note falling flat among one of many musicians within an orchestra. Just who's playing that "bad" note may be in question, but one thing is certain: Something isn't quite right here!

I wasn't certain what was amiss or wrong with Scientology, as my spiritual discernment and ability to distinguish between what is of God and what isn't - was surely lacking to say the least. After years of doing drugs, and hanging around with people who for the most part weren't very spiritual, unless you consider listening to the Beatles latest album while stoned on LSD a spiritual achievement; my level of discernment was at rock bottom.

That being said, let me suffice to say, while my spiritual senses were very dull, they weren't entirely unplugged... I was able to pick up a clue here and there through the day that gave me pause – that made me examine everything around me.

The conscience is a wonderful thing when it's working ... but it can become seared, and so ignored that it no longer keeps us alert to dangers and snares in our path and all around us. Thankfully, my conscience was still working and it would jar me out of my numb existence as I shuffled through the day at the org.

Perhaps my background as a Catholic and the time I spent studying some of the basic tenets of Christianity while going to a parochial school for a short time helped me see more clearly; to see the cracks and flaws in Scientology. Then again, I've often thought it was someone praying for me – my mother, or someone – somewhere who was interceding for a lost soul like me.

The more time I spent working in Detroit, watching and hearing those who were supposed to be the models of what Scientology could do for human beings; the more I was certain it was all a big lie – a hoax that I had bought into hook, line, and sinker... Slowly but surely I was starting to realize I had made a big mistake getting involved with Scientology.

I was not a godly or saintly man – not by a long shot. I was lost from a biblical point of view, but I did have a basic idea of what virtue and integrity were. My few years as a sincere convert to Christianity years earlier, and my limited exposure to the scriptures and some of the basic teachings of the Christian faith came into play here.

Hearing off color jokes and raunchy remarks from my fellow Scientologists during regular working hours at the org(only when patrons weren't present), was unsettling and seemed inappropriate for a number of reasons. First, I expected more professional behavior from an organization that was out to "save the world."

Secondly, I was taken back by the fact that once again, as with my experience with the lowly street people, and the rich and famous rock stars; here I found the same base, disgusting behavior that is common to all of us as humans – namely: sin and iniquity in full display.

Thankfully, I had enough biblical background(though it was very shallow to be sure), to know that cursing and telling dirty jokes was not a virtuous thing to do. To be frank, I honestly expected more from those on staff, especially the leaders in the org. This was only the tip of the iceberg.

Gossip, and derogatory comments about other staff members were fairly common, and the petty remarks that are often heard in almost any office today – were reminders to me that we weren't really any different from everyone else.

I was guilty of joining in at times, but not with any real enthusiasm. My hope was that Scientology – and the people who were espousing it's teachings were above that kind of crass and vulgar behavior.

Adultery and fornication, or cheating on your spouse was not a big deal as I soon discovered among those who were on staff. In fact the idea of being chaste or morally virtuous was not anything that anyone talked seriously about. The general attitude by most Scientologists in our org was if it's not really hurting anyone, if you're okay with it - and I'm okay with it; then it's okay. (more on that later)

Smoking at that time was tolerated, and the idea was that these bodies are just temporary facilities that we inhabit; so don't get to anxious about things like drinking alcohol or smoking cigarettes.

Because Scientology teaches their own version of "reincarnation", the idea of being overly concerned about just "one body among thousands", is not much to be worried about. That bothered me and didn't sound right.

The Bible & Me

Call it a "wooing" - or simply a strong pull on my inner being to read the Holy Bible; but one thing is certain: I knew that the answers I was looking for, was hoping for – would probably be found in that book!

I don't know where I obtained a Bible; because it was not a book held in high esteem, and I never saw anyone reading one or even referring to it – unless it was in derogatory terms. I remember having a sense of desperation – not unlike a man lost at sea; simply looking anywhere and everywhere for a way out, for a way to safety...

Years later, I learned that it was the Holy Spirit leading me, guiding me and directing me to go to the scriptures for the help and wisdom I needed at that time of my life. Someone or others somewhere were praying for me – of that I have no doubt.

Eventually, I did find a Bible, but now my problem was when and where to read it? That sounds like a small problem, but in that oppressive environment where your every move was closely monitored – was in fact a major obstacle.

I had to figure out how to read the Bible without others around me knowing, or being ridiculed and harassed were certainly going to be what I would have to endure. My reading of scriptures would be a game of "sneak a peek", whenever I had a few minutes to be alone – away from anyone's watchful eyes. The bathroom, was one place I could read for a few minutes.

My Bible, as I remember it was really just a New Testament, and a small one at that. There was no way I could conceal a large Bible, and besides – it was easy to carry with me without being noticed. The game was on, and I became very good at pulling out my small New Testament, and reading a few verses at a time and thinking about them.

This gave me great comfort and relief as I became more and more detached from the inner workings within the Org. there in Detroit. A separation was taking place on the inside of me; and the line was being drawn in my heart.

Fear & Faith

A funny thing began to happen to me after weeks of reading the scriptures. I began to be less and less afraid of what the other staff members might think of me, or what they were probably already thinking.

My faith in God and the words of Jesus Christ was growing day by day – and slowly I began to sense I was being set free from the world of darkness I was lost and trapped in. My exodus was on the horizon.

The gospels of Matthew, Mark, Luke and John had a profound on me – especially the gospel of John. I devoured the words of Jesus Christ, and they penetrated deep into my soul – speaking life to me in those dark weeks and months preceding my final departure from Scientology.

I remember crying out to God in my spirit, not out loud of course – but in my mind, quietly in my thoughts. I would tell God I needed to know the truth, I needed to know what to do? The beautiful thing is that God heard the cry of my heart, and the anguish of my soul.

While I never heard God's audible voice, I did hear God speaking to me in the scriptures as I read them; and as a whisper to me in my inner most being. I was convinced after months of studying and reading the New Testament – that God was going to free me and help me leave Scientology.

Trying to explain why it was so difficult to leave, when in reality I was free to walk out at anytime if I had chosen to is not easy to explain. I was not in physical chains, or being restrained or held against my will; but I was most definitely "bound and chained" in my mind and spirit. I was a prisoner.

I just felt I couldn't walk away ... I was being held back by some kind of invisible power or force that would not release me or let me leave Scientology. I know now it was pure evil, demonic strongholds of the devil that were keeping me from walking away and breaking free from the grip Scientology had over me.

At that time, I was gripped by some strange fear, that can only be described as irrational and inexplicable; at least not in logical terms that most people would understand or accept.

I've since learned that "understanding evil ", is not readily understood or managed without God's help. To put it another way, I was in over my head and dealing with spiritual wickedness and demons of deception that I was really no match for. At least not in my own strength or power.

Pray, pray, pray...

I have to admit prayer was not something I knew much about, and it wasn't something I did – at least not on a regular basis. Although I did attend a parochial school for a while, and was familiar with prayer – that seemed like a million years ago at that time.

When I was in church we would sometimes kneel, and also recite corporate prayers together as a congregation. Those prayers, while sincere as I remember – were very formal and said at a time when my life was quite normal and predictable.

My situation now within the confines of the Detroit Org. , found me saying prayers with a sense of urgency and quiet desperation.... The prayers I was offering up to God were really cries for God to deliver me from the horrible situation and circumstances I felt hopelessly trapped in!

I'm sure I cried out to God hundreds of times during the long months before I finally had the courage to walk away from Scientology. My prayers were said quietly of course within my mind; as there was no way I could ever be caught or found praying.

I knew from my discussions about religion, and Christianity in particular; that praying would be ridiculed and mocked if anyone was found engaging in that activity. In a word, prayer was something that people did who were lacking spiritually, something that unenlightened people did outside of the world of Scientology.

I wasn't ashamed or embarrassed about my new found faith in the Bible and God; I just didn't want to argue or be confronted about that at the time.

That being said, my prayers were said hidden from anyone's eyes, and strictly between me and God and no one else. I should add that much of my prayer began to be me simply talking to God about my problems, and my situation. To be honest, they were very shallow and centered mostly on myself, and my desires and perceived needs at the time.

Praising God, thanking God, and worshiping God were not the focus of my prayers; sadly – I was wholly concerned about my pitiful plight and desire to be free. God was kindly disposed to my self centered prayers; and was patiently listening to me repeat the same requests and concerns over and over.

I am eternally grateful for God's tender affection and kindness towards me at that time of my life. I know now that God was always there, patiently listening to the cry of my heart. My prayers were simple, and filled with heartfelt emotion, and God allowed me to "vent" and share my deepest hurts and cares with Him.

If you the reader can relate to some of what I've shared here about my being emotionally crippled and unable to free myself from the darkness and situation I felt trapped in; you will find the next chapter filled with hope and forgiveness that the world simply cannot give.

MY EXODUS FROM SCIENTOLOGY

I use the term "exodus" because like the Hebrew slaves who finally walked out of Egypt to freedom – I felt like God was setting me free from a terrible nightmare that I was trapped in. Here are some of the things going on in my life just prior to my actually leaving Scientology.

The weeks and days just prior to my exodus from Scientology, were very dark days in many ways. First, there were the overwhelming emotions of fear and despair that I could never seem to shake. I had this foreboding sense of dread that was like a shadow always with me at all times.

Well, that's not exactly correct; I did find peace and comfort whenever I was able to be alone where I could read the scriptures... that seemed to be the only time I really felt relief from the constant feeling that I was hopelessly trapped.

I was trapped – but it was that sense of being caught up in something evil, something horrible; that pushed me forward to the day I would finally have the courage to leave. It's hard to describe the mental state I was in at that time, but I can say that the very idea of leaving Scientology – just walking away seemed like an unlikely scenario at the time.

Why, you might ask would it be so hard to just walk away, I mean on it's face – I admit that sounds so simple. The truth is it should be but, when you're dealing with spiritual wickedness, and demonic strongholds that are involved with religious cults, and counterfeit religions – it's not.

Unless you've been personally involved with a religious cult, or are someone who has engaged in deliverance ministry; it is hard to comprehend the invisible (yet very real) stronghold that Satan has on those trapped in these snares. I can only tell you, while my mind was telling me I could just walk away; there were voices in my head telling me "not to go."

I know now that those voices – were in fact – the voices of demons.

Ignorant of "spiritual warfare", and being young and inexperienced ; I was in way over my head and unable to see I had been seduced and ensnared by the wiles of the devil. In a word – I was trapped.

I didn't keep a diary, and it was years ago so I can't remember the exact day or time when I knew I could no longer stay involved with Scientology; but that day finally came. I just knew it was time – it was time for me to go.

Desperate and tired of living like a zombie in a world where nothing made any sense – where everyday seemed like an endless routine of sameness. The time finally arrived, and I made a decision – I'm going to leave Scientology, I'm going to get as far away from this as I can...

Now the battle within me and around me began to become more intense.

At this point, I was terrified at the very idea of walking away from Scientology; the fear was paralyzing – crippling - but God gave me the strength to fight through those fears and negative emotions. I know now that it was prayer, and reading the scriptures that gave me the courage and inward strength to break away from the world of darkness I was in.

I had no money to speak of; the truth was all of us on staff were working endless hours for 15 to 20 dollars a week, really! And, that wasn't enough money to save or really make any elaborate plans with. My plan wouldn't require a lot of money, just enough to get me back to Flint, which only a short distance from where the Scientology organization was located in Detroit.

I had arranged for some friends to pick me up in the morning while I was there at the org working. My plan was to go to the org. with the other staff members like I did everyday; and when my friends arrived in Detroit to pick me up – to simply walk out the door.

To say I was scared would be an understatement; I was in reality paranoid and yet at the same time - very excited at the thought of finally being free. The thought of being free from the drudgery and predictable routine that had become my normal life as a Scientologist – was the thing that gave me the strength to push on in spite of my irrational fears...

While my common sense and reasoning told me there was no need to be afraid or worried about leaving. After all, I knew my contract with Scientology (a five year contract); was illegal because I had forged my father's signature.

That knowledge, wasn't enough to keep me from experiencing horrible feelings of unspeakable fear and dread at "what might happen" to me if I tried to leave. The fear I experienced was real and tormented me inwardly, though I never let anyone know how I was really feeling inside.

Before I finally found the courage to actually walk away from Scientology, I had some real spiritual battles in my mind. I wasn't sure what might happen, but eventually the pain of staying there in Detroit at the org. became so intense; that I knew no matter how I felt or what might happen – I had to leave. Once I made that fateful decision; the only thing left for me to do was to plan my escape...

The Day of Deliverance

I don't remember all of the details of that day, but I do remember it being a bright sunny day, and feeling excited about the day of my deliverance finally arriving.

I had a ride arranged for me to drive me back to Flint (my hometown in Michigan); and even if they didn't show up I was dead set on leaving that day. To be absolutely honest, there wasn't a demon in hell that was going to keep me from walking away from that org – that prison I had been living in for the past year in Detroit.

I have to admit, the head administrator for the org in Detroit intimidated me. She had piercing blue eyes, and a no nonsense approach to talking to everyone regardless of the situation... The thought of being confronted by her was unsettling, and my hope was to leave without having to deal with her. She was in some sense, my greatest fear – the fear of facing her and having to confront her was something I wanted to avoid if at all possible.

Fortunately, that morning went as good as I could have hoped for. Sometime around noon as I recall, my ride from Flint arrived and without making my departure obvious to the staff working that day – I left abruptly and without saying anything to anyone.

I just walked out the front door and got in the car with my friends, and no one was following me – no one had really noticed I had left it seemed.

I remember being flooded with a sea of emotions as I walked out that door for the last time. It was like waking up from a really bad nightmare; only I wasn't dreaming – it was all very real.

Joy – pure joy filled my entire being – really! I didn't know what my future would be as I began my journey back to Flint; but I did know that my long struggle with Scientology's hold on me was over.

Well, at least I thought it was. A few months later, I would find out that Scientology was not going to make my departure easy... (more on that later)

I know how I felt when I was locked up in jail for seven days and finally released and set free; but it didn't come close to the feelings of happiness and relief that flooded my soul on that day. There was much about Scientology that I didn't know at that time; but I knew in my heart that it was not what I thought it was when I first was exposed to it.

Being on staff in Detroit, and seeing the inner workings of Scientology, and it's rotten fruit – convinced me that it was evil, and not of God.

My post Scientology studies of the Bible, and religious cults showed me clearly that God had delivered me from one of the slickest "scams" of the devil. Although I entered Scientology when I was very vulnerable and susceptible to it's promise of being totally free and happy. (that was their big "spiel") It didn't take me long to realize I had signed up for a ticket to hell.

I know now that it was my mother's prayers, and God's tender mercies and grace that broke the chains that held me in it's grip. That – and my own pursuit for the truth.

Now, I have to be candid and tell you the reader, that my life immediately following my departure from Scientology was not at all what you might imagine. If I have left you with the idea that I left Scientology as a Christian, and free from all the junk that had entangled me – that would be misleading. I was still unsettled in my faith, and still searching...

While it's true, my spiritual eyes had been opened, and I was free from the overwhelming stranglehold that had me bound in fear and torment as a Scientologist in way over my head... I was by no means free from my own sins, nor had I yet totally surrendered my life to Jesus Christ.

To be totally honest – I was not a Christian at the time I left Scientology.

I was certainly leaning towards the Christian faith for direction and spiritual guidance by way of the Bible and my prior experiences with Christianity growing up. That being said, I was not wholly committed to being a Christian, nor was I totally convinced that it was the only true path to God.

Although my intense involvement with Scientology had taught me many valuable lessons; I cannot say that I left with any clear idea of what I wanted to do with my life, or exactly what God or religion I was ready to give my life to.

While it's true, I turned to the Bible and sought refuge in the scriptures, and in prayers to God(although my concept of God was very vague); it didn't result in me leaving Scientology professing to be being a "Christian" at least not in the way most people think of one's profession of faith.

If I had to choose what religion or God I was looking to or "leaning towards" at that time in my life, I certainly would have pointed to the Bible and Christianity. Sadly, my commitment at that time was quite shallow, and based more on my emotions at that time of my life – than any deep convictions. That would come later.

This was a strange time for me – a time of transition – but to where?

While I was excited at being free from Scientology, inside there was still no real peace. That would come later, but for the next few months the sheer joy of coming out of Scientology was exhilarating. It reminded me of the same emotions I had when I walked out of jail in Lima, Ohio as a scared and wayward young man.

The raw emotions of finally being free – finally being able to move about without answering to anyone was just pure joy for the moment. It wasn't going to last, but at that time of my life knowing I was free from the chains of fear that held me as a member of Scientology really cannot be put into words.

I didn't know what I was going to do, or where I was going to stay; really I was starting all over with nothing. No home, no job, no money, and most of my friends were out of my life at that time. In a real sense, I was going to be starting my life all over again and oddly enough, I wasn't really upset or scared about that. Somehow I just knew things would end up working out. That was the way I had always been, I was born with a sense of optimism.

No matter what was ahead, I always felt I would be able to survive, and overcome whatever might come my way. I suppose that was my scratch and claw mentality, and my stubborn pride that refused to say, "I give up."

Being young has it's advantages for sure, and being blind to the real dangers and pitfalls that life can bring; may not spare you from it's consequences – but it can keep you from being paranoid with fear or unable to keep moving forward...   That was me at that time.

So I was free from Scientology, but still not ready to totally commit my life to God. I was slowly moving in the right direction – towards God and His way of doing things; but honestly there were still a few more lessons for me to learn before I completely surrendered everything to Jesus Christ. God was patient with me at that time, and was lovingly drawing me to Himself, but it would have to be my choice whether I would serve Him or not.

BACK TO THE SAME O SAME O...

As a dog returns to his own vomit, so a fool returns to his folly.

PROV. 26:11

It's funny how we gravitate to what we are comfortable with, and as the scripture above says, it wasn't long for me to go back once again to the things I was familiar with before I became involved with Scientology.

Drugs, rock & roll, and women were part and parcel of my years before being a Scientologist; and now that I was free from my entanglement with Scientology you would think my life would take a "straighter path"... that was simply not the case.

I stayed with my mother for a time, and that gave me time to get back in touch with my old friends. I still had this crazy dream of "making in in the music world" as a musician; but at that time of my life it meant starting over – which was not an easy task.

It didn't take me long to find like minded individuals with the same aspirations and goals as me – they were usually the same people who I would get high with. Getting high with other people was always a good way to find band mates, and it wasn't long before I had formed another band to launch my next attempt at being a "rock star".

So here I was back again, doing the same ol "song and dance" or the "same o same o" as people like to say. Getting high, staying up all night playing music with my fellow musicians, and not doing anything you might consider "spiritual"... The truth is I was right back where I had been prior to my joining Scientology. I was older and a little wiser to be sure, but in practical terms I was still living an unholy and ungodly lifestyle, and was a long way from being close to God.

Saved, Saved, Saved

Now what I'm about to share is bizarre to how most Christians view the subject of "salvation", but it is what actually happened to me – so I share it as best I can remember.

After coming back to my hometown (Flint,Michigan); I stayed with my mother and had my own room. I was reading the Bible, but was still smoking marijuana and listening to secular music, and much of it was far from being spiritually edifying or wholesome by most Christian standards.

 In a word, I was not saved, not praying, not going to church, not witnessing, and not thinking about God or spiritual things – at least not on any consistent basis. I hadn't even asked Jesus to be my Savior...

That was all about to change...

It wasn't long before I started hanging around with an old friend of mine, who dressed and looked like Jimi Hendrix. He even played the guitar left handed, with the guitar upside down like Hendrix. We were inseparable, and I dressed like an Englishman, with long hair; and we both wore clothes that said clearly: We are "rockers" looking for a party. Our lives revolved around music, drugs & women – that was it. My old ways resurfaced again.

We went to clubs, to concerts, and just hung out together smoking dope, and listening to music into the wee hours of the morning. It didn't take me long to jump back full speed into my old life style of partying and excess. There was one big difference with me at this time. I was pretty bored with everything I was doing. I was going through the motions, but my heart wasn't into it anymore.

The drugs, music, and even the one night stands with some girl who I just met hours early were not exciting me anymore – as B.B. King had so aptly said in one of his classic blues songs: "The thrill is gone baby." Yes indeed, the thrill of getting high, and partying; none of it was bringing me any real happiness or joy. In my heart of hearts – I knew that there was more to life than just getting high and girls and rock and roll music.

I was at a point in my life where God, or the idea of God was very attractive to me. I was still reading the Bible on and off, and it was because of that, and my mother's prayers; that I was seriously thinking about my life, and what life in general is all about.

Now you would think after all I had been through with my time in Scientology, my time being immersed in the secular rock culture, and my time living on the streets as a vagabond – I would be more than ready to come to Jesus. But sadly, I was still holding on to some of the pleasures and things I still loved – like getting high, chasing women, and partying with the wild crowd regularly.

I finally did come to the point where I was exhausted by living in the fast lane, and doing the same things I'd been doing for the last several years. After some serious soul searching and reflection; I began to once again dig into the Bible and think seriously about God. It wasn't long after this period of my life, that I finally was ready – ready to get right with God.

Saved In My Mother's Kitchen

Now my mother lived in an up stair's apartment, which was very small and ordinary by most standards. The kitchen was simple, and a nice place to hang out when we had the "munchies" which is a state of physical hunger that is common to anyone who is familiar with being stoned on marijuana.

On one particular evening after smoking some dope, my friend and I went into the kitchen to look for anything to satisfy our craving for food... We turned on a portable black & white T.V. set there in the kitchen, and to our surprise Billy Graham was preaching a sermon at some big crusade.

We decided to have a few laughs, and watch him preach while we ate and amused ourselves for a few minutes. What happened in the next few minutes was life changing – at least it was for me.

I don't remember the title of the sermon Billy Graham preached, and most of the words have faded over time into oblivion. But, I do remember the part at the end where he talked about there being a heaven and a hell, and that I could be with Jesus in heaven and avoid hell; if I would give my life to Jesus Christ.

He went on to ask those of us at home to make a decision to accept Jesus as their personal Savior, and to confess we are all sinners who needed to be saved, or words similar to that...

I don't remember my exact prayer, but I do remember kneeling down there on the kitchen floor and asking God to forgive me, and to save me. I asked Jesus Christ to be my Savior, and inside of me something happened – something wonderful that is hard to put into words.

I felt as though a heavy dark cloud had been lifted off of me. I felt clean inside and light through and through my entire being. I got up on my feet, and I was completely sober and in my right mind. Any influence that drugs had over me was gone – completely gone!

I knew right then that I was saved. I knew that my sins had been forgiven and that I was a different person. I was changed on the inside, and it was like a great light had been turned on within me, I was glowing inside – I felt like a new person. I can say that I was "born again."

Jesus answered and said to him, "Most assuredly, I say to you, unless one is born again, he cannot see the kingdom of God." **JN.3:3**

Losing A Friend

My best friend (who dressed like Jimi Hendrix), knelt down with me and prayed with me in my mother's kitchen. It felt great knowing we were both committing our lives to God at the same time. It was surreal – I mean one minute we were stoned out in my mom's kitchen just drifting through life without any real aim or purpose, and now we were "saved" and in a whole new world.

I was thrilled and excited that we were embarking on this journey together – it was a very special time for both of us, and I was happy I was sharing this experience with my best friend at that time.

That was to be short-lived...

Within a few days, I was surprised to find out that Lenny didn't want to get together with me. I didn't think much about it, but finally after being put off for a few days; I decided to go and visit him to confront him about his cool attitude towards me.

When I finally arrived at his apartment, I began to ask Lenny why he was avoiding me, and acting so strange; I mean after all we were best friends – and we had just both prayed to God to save us. We had just committed our lives to Jesus Christ, and now Lenny was acting very cold and distant towards me. That hurt, but I had to confront him to know what he was really thinking.

Lenny told me, he couldn't give up his girlfriend he was staying with(she was paying his rent and supporting him); and he wasn't ready to give up his marijuana and lifestyle yet. By lifestyle, he meant the bars, the loose sex, the illegal drugs, and other things that were all part of the rock and roll culture we were both immersed in.

I understood Lenny's excuses, but I was not in any mood to accommodate his lack of commitment to Christ. I was furious, and gave Lenny a rebuke that can only be described as a "get behind me Satan" kind of assault on him. A verbal onslaught of spiritual superiority, that years later I would acknowledge as "truth spoken without love." Not a good way to end our friendship to say the least.

My new found passion and love for God, the Bible and my new path as a Christian made me very harsh and judgmental towards my friend Lennie. I regret the way I talked to him, but I don't regret my zeal for Christ – just the way I reacted that day.

I remember feeling betrayed, and all alone. I actually shook the "dust off of my feet" and railed a curse of some kind on Lenny as I marched off down the street mumbling to myself. My best friend at that time had let me down, and left me to face this new journey with God by myself. I was feeling quite alone, and angry that Lenny was so weak and lacking in his commitment.

Regardless of how I felt about Lenny's retreat, and refusal to go on with his walk with Christ, I was determined not to let that keep me from walking with God and following through with my initial decision to follow Jesus Christ. Little did I know how rough the next year would be, and how badly I would fare as a follower of Christ.

Going Backwards...

The next few months after I was saved in my mother's kitchen were very weird, even for someone who was used to being in weird situations. I didn't have any real Christian friends, and I didn't have a church or Christians around me to mentor or advise me on what the Christian life is supposed to be like, or how Christians are to conduct themselves.

I did read the Bible, and I was sincerely trying to walk with God, albeit my knowledge and understanding of God was feeble at best, and I was not attending church services anywhere. The spiritual foundation in my life at that time was filled with plenty of sincere emotions and intentions; but was sorely lacking in substance or doctrinal integrity.

Without spiritual guidance, and lacking any real doctrinal or theological foundation; I was slowly being drawn back to the world of music, sex, and drugs that I was familiar with... Once again I found myself longing to be in a band, and to be with people who loved secular music as much as I did.

That was easy, before long I was again back to my old ways. I moved out of my mother's house, mostly because it wasn't conducive to my dream of playing music in a band, and it was much too restrictive for my undisciplined life – staying up late and playing my guitar and music; something my mother could never put up with.

By this point, you may be thinking – why couldn't I stay focused, more committed to Christ? Why couldn't I live a more godly and holy life? Why was I so quick to revert back to my old lifestyle of drugs, secular rock music, and everything else I had walked away from?

Good questions, and the answer is simply I was not letting Jesus Christ be the Lord of my life. I was saved but going backwards with no clue as to how I could stop myself from returning once again to the things I knew God hated, things I knew Christians aren't supposed to be doing. The problem was I seemed powerless to keep myself from going back to the things that God had saved me from.

To be sure, this was a real dilemma for me spiritually because inside I knew that I needed to make a clean break from everything that was part of my old lifestyle of non-stop partying and getting stoned. The battle to go forward all the way with Christ, or just live somewhere in the middle – waffling back and forth was always going on.

At that time, my lack of total commitment to Jesus robbed me of any real peace. My conscience was always reminding me that I was falling short, and needed to stop playing around with my faith. I knew God was calling me to live a holy and consecrated life ; to stop doing the same old things that Jesus died to save me from – but my flesh was not so keen on surrendering to the will of God.

LOOSE GOOSE

Band names are crazy and unusual as most people can attest. Our band's name was zany and funny even for back then, somehow we ended up choosing the name: Loose Goose. You have to admit it has a certain ring to it. (Okay you can stop giggling right now).

We were a seven piece band, with the lofty goal of learning about 25 to 30 top 40 songs, or "cover songs" as they are called. We had a female singer, and I was the lead male singer and bassist for the band.

We were practicing about 3 days a week together, and were making great progress towards having our songs and stage show ready for the bars in our area.

Now, I have to share at this point that my heart was not into being a "bar band" and it was not where I really wanted to play. The idea of playing for people stoned and drunk in a smoky bar, who really didn't come to see the band(at least not as the main reason); was not my idea of being successful as a rock musician.

My real dream was to be a "touring band" like the Rolling Stones, or the BYRDS, or The CREAM, etc. Those bands commanded respect, and people came out to see them because of the music they played, and the shows they put on.

But you have to pay your dues, and I was not done paying my dues by a long shot. I knew that being a successful bar band, was a stepping stone that most great bands and musicians had to travel before they made it to the big time. So, I worked hard to make sure our band was professional and at the top of our game. We were close to reaching that goal, when something happened that would change my life forever.

Now, let me remind you that about a year earlier, I had gotten saved in my mother's kitchen. I have no doubt that I was truly saved at that time, but I'm also certain that I had drifted right back into my old sinful lifestyle. I was mellower, and not as wild; but I was still smoking, cursing, and pursuing my own desires and dreams without much thought of God or others for that matter.

Now without going into deep theology, there are those who believe "once saved – always saved"; and there are others who teach you can walk away from God and go back into a life of sin and go to hell. In essence "become unsaved."

I'll admit I'm in the latter group, though I believe it's a very difficult and hypersensitive subject to talk about with most Christians. That being said, the scriptures are clear that it's possible to "abandon the faith", and that saved individuals can neglect their salvation.

I have my own thoughts on that, but one thing was clear – I was going backwards and away from God after my initial experience of giving my life to Jesus in my mother's kitchen.

I was moving further away from my love and zeal for God and the Bible, and I was slowly going right back to my old ways. I believe I was still saved, and had I died I would have gone to heaven. I was a sloppy and undisciplined Christian to be sure, but I had not denied Christ or stopped trusting in Him to save me.

Unknown to me at the time, I was about to be faced with some important decisions about "who would be in control of my life." Up to that time, I was simply drifting along with no real power or ability to live a godly life... The truth was I had no knowledge or understanding about who Jesus Christ really is!

I definitely knew I was saved – that was settled and I knew Jesus was my personal Savior. What I didn't know was Jesus wanted me to know Him as my Lord – my King, - and my best friend.

The page was about to be turned on my journey with God, and I would never be the same ever again. Looking back I marvel at how weak and carnal I had become after asking Jesus to save me. I know now – what I didn't know then; that trying to live as a Christian without knowing Christ as Lord of all – is not going to work.

I'm convinced that many Christian's today are living lives of frustration and constant defeat and spiritual setbacks, because they have never relinquished control of their lives to Jesus Christ as their Lord. That was my problem, I wanted Jesus to be my Savior, and He was; but I wasn't ready to surrender every area of my life to Him as Lord of my life – all of it.

God was waiting patiently for me – and finally the time had come for me to decide who was going to be in charge of my life. Let me share with you what happened to me during this shaky and confusing time as a new Christian in need of God's help.

JESUS AS LORD

I wasn't a hardened sinner, and I was not the same man I was before I gave my life to Christ – that was a fact. The problem was I wasn't living for Jesus Christ in my daily walk. I wasn't praying, reading the Bible, or going to church, or witnessing, or doing any of the things that normally accompany a Christian's life and intimate walk with God.

I knew Jesus Christ as my personal Savior, but sadly – I didn't know Jesus as my Lord. That was about to change.

For months after asking Jesus to be my Savior, I had drifted spiritually and admittedly I was getting weaker and weaker as the days went by. God saw my pitiful condition, and stepped in to take me where I couldn't go without His help. The rest of this story is how God had me back up and do things over again, by that I mean "do them over the right way."

I was living in a house with some of our band members in downtown Flint, Michigan. We would stay up late jamming on our instruments, or partying, and sleep in late into the afternoon before waking up to do it all over again.

On one cold winter day, I heard a knock on the front door. I remember trying to ignore it, in hopes it would stop and the person would go away.

The knocking kept on going on and on, until finally I had enough of that. I got up, after throwing on some clothes and went downstairs to see who was banging on our front door.

Wow! To my surprise it was my sister Bobbi – she was standing there smiling at me, and glowing from ear to ear. She was radiant with a sparkle and gleam in her eyes that made me very happy for her. I knew she had been having some personal problems, and to see her so clear eyed, and composed had a very strong impact on me as we stared into each other's eyes.

After she came in and sat down; she looked at me and stated in a no nonsense manner, "Terry and I got saved." I knew what she meant, but I asked her to explain what happened to her and Terry her husband. She was quick to share her testimony of how God had saved her from her problem with drugs, and other things in her life; and that Terry was saved too.

She said they were going to church and their whole family was now Christians. Her face was shining and her countenance and appearance was such that it was in stark contrast to the sadness and tension that I had often seen on her face in the past. She was different; that was for certain; and she was telling me that it was Jesus Christ who had changed her.

I believed her. I believed her because months earlier I had experienced a similar change myself on the inside. I had slowly drifted back into my old lifestyle, but I knew that what she was telling me was real.

God had sent Bobbi my sister to my home in order to help me. I needed guidance and Christians to teach me and assist me in my journey with God; and Bobbi my sister was all part of that plan. I knew in my heart that Bobbi's visit was by "divine appointment"; but as is often the case it was not going to be simple. Life is often complicated as was the case with me.

Bobbi told me that there was "revival" at there church that week, and she wanted me to go that night with her to the meeting. I told her that was impossible because our band had arranged for an audition with a Booking agent from New York, who was going to start booking us at clubs in our area. I told her as the leader of the band – I just couldn't cancel our audition at the last minute.

Bobbi, was undeterred, and said she would pray for God to make it happen, or allow for me to go. I was surprised at her show of faith, and told her, "It will take a miracle for me to be able to go." Right after that, the phone rang and it was our organ player saying he had smashed his hand in the car the night before and wouldn't be able to go and play.

I told my sister, that won't keep us from going. We can still play without him. Just then, the phone rang again. This time it was the club owner where the audition was to be held, telling us that the Booking agent from New York had just canceled our audition.

Wow! That was God and I knew it. I looked at my sister, and told her that was God and I would go with her to the revival that night. God had answered her prayers, and mine as well.

Some Unfinished Business

It's funny how bumpy and strange my first year was with the Lord after first praying for God to save me, and asking Jesus to be my Savior. Without any real solid Biblical teaching, and little to no spiritual guidance or mentoring in my life; I was reaping what I was sowing. My life was filled with bad habits, little discipline, and no real spiritual foundation. I was drifting along day by day and going farther and farther away from God.

I believe my soul was saved, my spirit had been born again, but sadly my flesh was ruling my life, and I was about as spiritual as a scarecrow in an empty field in the middle of January. Not much fruit in my life, and I'm sure no one around me would have known I was a Christian by the way I was living.

I said all that to say that God saw my pitiful condition, and knew exactly what I needed. I needed to take care of a couple of things in my life, before I could go on in my spiritual walk with God. I won't preach a sermon here, but I will say God allows us to go forwards or backwards — the choice is ours to make.

Whenever we say "yes" to God as He speaks to us(no matter how that may be), we go forward in our walk and relationship with Him. Whenever we say "no" to God, no matter how that situation may arise – we go backwards.

I won't go into deep theology here on the subject and questions surrounding "salvation" that Christians argue about. But, I will say I for one think going forward is a much more prudent thing to do, and I do not want to find out what happens when we go backwards in a consistent pattern of disobedience. Hmm – not wise wouldn't you agree?

So, I go the revival that night with my sister Bobbi, and my other sister Sandy is there with us. I remember a young evangelist named Paul was preaching a message about heaven and hell, and at the end of his sermon he gave an invitation to ask Jesus to save you and be your Savior.

I practically ran forward that night, as I was under heavy conviction by The Holy Spirit to take care of two things in my life that were sins in my life. I knew I had asked God to save me months earlier and I believed that God had saved me and forgiven me of my sins.

There was only one big problem, actually two big problems.

The First Thing...

I had not forgiven my father for what I thought he had done to me in making me leave home as a teen to live alone on the streets. I had anger and bitterness towards my dad for making me beg and steal and lie and walk the streets cold and hungry. I was holding all of this anger and resentment in my heart towards my father.

I hadn't forgiven my father, and up to that point in time; I was still holding unforgiveness in my heart towards him. God was speaking to my heart as I knelt there at the altar – and telling me in no uncertain terms that "I HAD TO FORGIVE MY FATHER." The voice in my heart was clear and strong.

I wrestled with that in my heart and mind for the longest time, and when I looked around I could see many people all around me praying for me and others who had knelt to pray for salvation and other needs.

Later I found out that I was praying there for probably an hour and a half, with many people staying right there with me helping me pray through...

There was a spiritual war going on in my soul, and the saints around me were praying with me and for me. I will always be eternally grateful for those Christians who were praying for me as I struggled within over the emotions that were boiling within me.

I remember kneeling at the altar, and hearing God say to me. "YOU HAVE TO FORGIVE YOUR FATHER MICHAEL." There was no sermonizing, no scriptures read to me, just the simple admonition and command: FORGIVE YOUR FATHER!

I got that message, and I finally relented and surrendered my will to God – and forgave my father from my heart. As I did, I felt God wash through my entire being with a cleansing power and force that is indescribable. It can best be described as being filled with a "love" that goes beyond words. I suddenly was filled with a wonderful and new love for my father.

Immediately, my attitude and feelings towards my dad changed, in an instant! God allowed me to see my father the way He saw him, broken and weak – a poor man without God in His life. I now was ready to embrace and love my father in spite of what he might have done or didn't do towards me. God changed me, though my father was still the same man.

"For if you forgive men their trespasses, your heavenly Father will also forgive you. 15 But if you do not forgive men their trespasses, neither will your Father forgive your trespasses. **Mt.6:14-15**

The Second Thing...

The other thing that was in my life that God had convicted me of that evening was the "idol of music" in my heart. I knew my love for music was strong, but God revealed to me that it was a "god" and "idol" that I had to repent of – something that I had to let go of – something that I had to give completely to God.

I'm not sure which of these two things were a bigger problem, my "unforgiveness" towards my father; or my worship of music? They were both very different, but God showed me that evening that to go on with my relationship with Him – I would have to deal with both of these issues. That was not going to be easy.

I went back and forth from my problem with my father, to my idol of music. I knew God was telling me I had to repent of both of these two sins. One thing was certain in my mind, I had to either deal honestly with both of these issues that night; or walk out of that church and hold on to these two "dark clouds" that were in my heart.

God was not forcing me to choose; but He was letting me know that saying no to what He wanted and expected me to do would be "disobedience". I don't know what might have happened if I had said no to God, but I didn't want to find out.

I remember God showing me how I worshiped music, and how it was a "god" in my life. I thought about music almost every waking hour of my life, and spent untold hours either listening to, or making music on some instrument like the guitar or harmonica... From the time I woke up – until the time I went to sleep I was consumed with thoughts about music, songs, bands, lyrics, melodies, concerts, on and on - music was more than my best friend – it was a god in my life that had to go.

Okay, I confessed to God there on the floor as I knelt before God, yes I've made music a god, and I repent of that. I give you my music, I give you all my musical gifts, talent, everything – I give it all to you. I can't remember my exact words – but those words are pretty close to what I told God as I prayed there at that altar.

God heard me.

When I got up, I knew that I would never be the same. I was saved to the deepest part of my being. While I may have been saved months earlier, God was not going to allow me to walk in darkness and claim to be saved. I was working out my salvation in steps...

I can't explain it fully, but I can tell you this. I don't think I would have been saved had I walked out of that church without "forgiving my father" or "repenting of the idol/god that music" was in my life.

Little children, keep yourselves from idols.   **1 JN.5:21**

HARD CHOICES

And do not be conformed to this world, but be transformed by the renewing of your mind, that you may prove what is that good and acceptable and perfect will of God. **Rom.12:2**

When that night was over, I had some difficult decisions to make. I knew I had to leave the band, and that playing in bars and pursuing my dream of being in a secular band was over. Everything was now clear to me – I had to make some changes in my life, and no matter how difficult or problematic they might be - I had to make some hard choices.

My first decision was obvious; I had to quit the band and as the leader/founder of the band – I had to inform everyone I was leaving and tell them why. I owed them all that. We had all invested months of money/time and effort into our goal of being a successful club/bar band; and now I was walking away from our commitment to each other.

For me, that wasn't very hard because I knew that playing secular music was no longer an option for me as a Christian, and besides, I never really was keen on being in a bar band. Personally, I thought it was not that great an achievement to say I play in a bar band. It wasn't a big deal to me.

The most awkward part of that whole episode, was explaining to the band that I had been "saved" and could no longer play in a bar band, nor did I wish to for that matter. That caused some of them to be angry with me, or at least baffled by my sudden conversion to Christianity. Strange reactions, and awkward moments were what I remember about that situation.

My Parting Gift

Now I have to share an amusing, though rather sad incident that happened at the time I left the band. This is one of those events that happen in your life that you never forget, and always sticks in your mind. I learned a lot about myself and my friend Frank, and share this experience hoping you profit from my recollection of it.

Frank, was our guitar player. He had long curly white hair and a beard. He was an excellent lead guitarist, and a formidable musician in every respect. He always was after my Gibson Les Paul Junior(not unlike the guitar used by the band's guitarist in MOUNTAIN). He coveted that guitar, and would often ask if he could buy it or get it from me... my answer was always a quick "no." It was obvious he "coveted" my guitar – and that made me enjoy saying no to him all the more...

Well, after I was touched by God at my sister's church, and delivered from my sins as I outlined earlier, I had the strongest desire to witness my new found faith in Christ to Frank.

I decided to give the guitar, my Les Paul Junior to Frank with no strings attached – just give it to him free and clear! So one day that's exactly what I did.

Now Frank was standing there, and I said, "Hey Frank, I want to share something with you." "Yeah, what's that" Frank said. "Well, you know I told you that Jesus Christ saved me, right?" And Frank is looking at me with this funny glare, wondering where am I going with this...

"Well Frank, I want you to know how real Jesus Christ is to me, and just how real this all is to me." Franks still staring at me. "Here Frank, I'm giving you this guitar, as a witness to you - to let you know that I love Jesus Christ more than this guitar. And you know how much I loved this guitar, don't you?"

Frank literally fell back on his butt, and with the guitar in his hands, and him looking up at me - was totally speechless. I was delighted to see Frank so blown away by my giving him that guitar. It was for me a very special moment, I knew right then and there that I was free from my slavery to music as an idol.

That simple act of giving Frank my guitar set me free, really free. It showed him, me, everyone; Mick(my nickname) loves God more than that guitar. It was just one small deed, but it was a huge step for a man who previously worshiped music and guitars in particular. I was a free man! Free from my worship of music.

The Saddest Thing

Have you ever had something happen to you that rocks you to the core of your being? I mean shakes you down to the depths of your very soul. Well, this story has a weird ending, and it's not pretty or beautiful – it's very sad and tragic.

Months later, after leaving the band, and moving out of the house where we all lived and practiced. It was also after I had given Frank my Les Paul Jr. guitar that he had always coveted and wanted...

Well, I was downtown, near where we had all lived; and just happened to be walking down the sidewalk when I saw Frank walking down the other side of the street; across from me.

We both glanced at each other, and I waved and called out to Frank, "Hey Frank, hey Frank – how are you?" Nothing, no response or reaction, he acted like he didn't even see me. Strange, I'm thinking. So I called out his name again, but this time Frank was actually running away from me!

I stopped dead in my tracks, and I heard the Lord speak to me as clear as a bell: "Frank thinks you want the guitar back that you gave him." That hit me hard, I stopped dead in my tracks. I remember thinking 'Frank is running away from me because he's afraid I'm going to ask for my guitar back.' My heart was broken – really. After all, we were the best of friends; or so I thought at the time.

I shouted out to Frank, "Frank, I don't want the guitar back, it's yours forever! - I don't want the guitar it was a gift to you." He never looked back and kept running away. I was saddened beyond belief; I could hardly believe my eyes. My dear friend, put his love for a guitar above his love and affection for me. The pain I felt standing there cannot be put into words.

Now I knew how God must feel when we love things more than Him, and run away from Him as He calls out our name. I learned many lessons that day about "love, idols, and things" that come before our relationship and love for God.

At the time of this writing I've never again seen or heard from Frank. My hope and prayer is that he has come to know Jesus Christ as his own personal Lord and Savior.

Don't Make Me Choose

When I first began my journey with Jesus Christ as my personal Savior and then later "Lord" of my life; I had no idea how much it was going to cost me... but I was soon to find out.

I had been seriously involved with a beautiful girl, Cathy*for about 2 years just prior to my conversion to Christianity. She and I were both party animals and had a lot in common.

We both liked to get stoned on drugs, and listen to rock & roll music. We were in love and both thought being engaged was the next logical step in our relationship.

Her father owned a tool company in Jackson Michigan, and they would let me stay with them and actually spend the night in her bedroom alone. They were very well to do, but also liberal even by the moral standards of most American families at that time.

That surprised me. Her dad and brother invited both of us out to a bar/grill where we began to talk and get to know one another better. I had the feeling both of them were sizing me up to see if I was an acceptable guy to be hooked up with their daughter/sister.

I'm not sure if I was getting a passing grade or not, but drinking alcohol is not my forte... I think Cathy, my girlfriend at the time was holding her liquor better than me. On that count, I was probably getting a failing grade.

So plans were being made to get married, but we still did not have a set date for that, we were content to just drift along in that phase of our relationship. Hmm – but then a funny thing happened.

I got saved! I mean really saved - I was no longer the "old Mick!" I hadn't changed much on the outside, but inside I was totally changed – and it felt good – it felt really good.

I was soon to find out that my fiance was not ready for such a drastic change. What happened next was like getting slapped in the face, only worse – it hurt me in the deepest part of my heart and soul.

When I told my fiance I had given my life to Christ, that I was now a Christian she was silent. Nothing – she wouldn't answer my phone calls or my letters to her. Just silence. That hurt me really bad and let me know – following Jesus came with a price.

So looking back on that time of my life, I have to say that the joy and peace I had been looking for all my life was shaken; but still very much present. That fact alone stands out in my mind. Really – having my fiance dump me like a sack of rotten potatoes without so much as a whisper; should have rocked my world.

It was not a happy time for sure, but my commitment to Christ was rock solid even at that stage of my walk with God. No matter what, I wasn't going to go back... I wasn't going to turn around and go back to the way things were before I met Christ. No way Jose!

I just decided: If you are going to make me choose – between Jesus and something else. YOU LOSE! That expression, my wife can tell you has become my mantra or slogan as I journey through my life down here on earth. Don't make me choose – or you will lose.

I don't know what happened with my fiance Cathy after we parted ways; but I do know she didn't forget about me. A couple of years later, after I had married my lovely wife Debbie I was home taking a bath when I heard my wife talking to someone on the phone upstairs. "No, don't call back, he's married now to me." I asked my wife, "Who was that?" to which she replied that was a girl named Cathy asking to speak to you.

"I told her you're married now to me, and not to call back." I was amused and curious at the same time. I knew my wife was a little upset about that, but still I was thinking to myself, "what did she want? Maybe she's a Christian now and wants to tell me that... " A few minutes later the phone rang again, and it was Cathy again wanting to talk to me.

This time my wife was not going to let that happen. I heard her say very loudly – "He's married to me, so don't you ever call back again!" I was proud of my wife for showing such passion and love for me. Still, there was a part of me that wanted to know how Cathy was doing, and what had happened to her since we last saw each other. Some things are better left alone; and I'm happy to say – that was the end of that.

The irony in this whole episode is that our engagement was sealed with me giving Cathy a beautiful cross that she wore. It only goes to show that wearing a cross as a piece of jewelry is not at all what it means to "take up the cross" and follow Jesus. I don't know what she did with that cross I gave her, but I truly hope that my testimony (I shared that at length in my letters to her), and that small cross caused her to turn her life over to the Lord. That is my prayer.

Saying Goodbye...

Therefore "Come out from among them And be separate, says the Lord. Do not touch what is unclean, And I will receive you." **2 CO.6:17**

Saying goodbye to my band mates, and friends I had at that time wasn't really that hard for me; it was just something that I knew I had to do if my walk with God was going to really last. I didn't need anyone to tell me, "Mike you need to quit the band – you need to change your lifestyle."

Some things in life – like smoking, and drinking too much alcohol, or looking at pornography, don't require anyone telling us "that's not good for us." That was the case with me when it came to the ungodly lifestyle I was living. I knew in my heart of hearts – that for there to be any lasting change in my life. Some hard decisions would have to be made.

The good news was – at that point in my life – I was ready to change... It's been said, "When the pain of staying the same is greater than the pain to change – you will change." How true.

I had struggled in my walk as a Christian my first year, and knowing Jesus Christ as both my Savior and Lord made all the difference in the world. I knew that God was real, and I believed in a literal hell and heaven; but that wasn't enough to keep me from drifting back to my old way of thinking and living.

Finding out that Jesus had to be "Lord of all," or not Lord at all – was a painful lesson that my first year as a floundering young Christian had taught me. This time, I knew for my walk with Christ to be successful; it would mean not only saying goodbye to my friends who were still partying and getting stoned to the wee hours of the morning.

It meant I would have to do a 180, or turn around and go in the opposite direction that I head been going prior to coming to Christ. This was going to be radical to the max. This is true "<u>repentance</u>" and step one for anyone who is truly saved or desiring to be saved.

While many people think of the exterior when they think of "changing" - like cutting one's hair, or the way one dresses or looks on the outside; God had something much more challenging than that for me.

God was going to change me from the inside out, but for me that also meant putting myself into a totally different environment... it meant moving into a place where I wouldn't be surrounded by the temptations and vices that were a normal part of my everyday life.

My entire lifestyle revolved around drugs, sex, and rock & roll. Those 3 things were the "gods" in my life, and that meant I needed to put myself in a place where I wasn't tempted by the things that had become chains that held me captive.

Admittedly, I was an addict to those three things; and to be free I needed to remove myself, and anything that would come between my relationship with Jesus Christ.

My journey to "spiritual freedom" was two fold: First, move away from anyone or anything that would drag me back to a lifestyle that was ungodly and contrary to the teachings of Jesus Christ. Secondly, to put myself into an environment that would allow me to grow spiritually in my walk with God.

The first part of this process(the bible calls it sanctification), was simply a matter of cutting myself off from my old friends, and moving out of the house and area where I had been staying. That part was easy because my sister, Bobbi allowed me to move in with her right after I had recommitted my life to Jesus as Lord.

The second phase of my spiritually quest to be totally free from my old ways – my old lifestyle of excess and lawlessness; was not so easy. This would mean changing the way I think, the way I speak or talk, the way I act.

I was soon to find out that real inward change, would take more than just moving from one location to another – no matter how safe and relatively temptation free that place might be.

What I needed most, was nothing I could find here, or do myself – it was someone that I needed. Someone that would help me, be with me, and lead and guide me into all truth.

The "GAME CHANGER"

On January 4th, 1973 I asked God to fill me with His Holy Spirit, and that same night I was baptized with the Spirit of God and the power I needed to live a godly and righteous life before God and man was now residing in me!

The difference that made in my walk with God cannot be adequately put into words, but it was a "game changer" in the truest sense of the word. Having the Holy Spirit with me – in me – and guiding me everyday; has allowed me to overcome my flesh and the temptations that come my way with power and with more consistency.

It has changed my walk with God forever. Without going into theology, let me simply say "being filled" with the Holy Spirit is something every born again Christian should seek and ask God for.

The only prerequisite for receiving the baptism of the Holy Spirit, is that a person first repent and ask Jesus to save them from their sins. In the next part of this book, is a short prayer for anyone that has not yet surrendered their life to Jesus Christ.

After a person has asked Jesus to be their Savior and Lord, it is the perfect time to ask God to fill you with The Holy Spirit. Trying to live a victorious life in our own strength without being filled with God's Spirit will mean our lives will lack the necessary power and unction to do the "greater works" that Jesus said His followers would do.

After being filled with The Spirit of God, our ability to overcome sin and temptation, and to be effective witnesses will be evident for all to see.

I encourage you to study these spiritual truths for yourself in the Bible, and desire all that God has for everyone who decides to follow Jesus

Christ. It is a true statement that – being saved is just the beginning! There is so much more – much more; and being filled (actually continuously being filled)is something that should be ongoing all the days of our lives here on earth.

LK.11:13   *If you then, being evil, know how to give good gifts to your children, how much more will your heavenly Father give the Holy Spirit to those who ask Him!"* (Jesus speaking)

EPH.5:18   *And do not get drunk with wine, for that is dissipation, but be filled with the Spirit,*

JN.16:13 *But when He, the Spirit of truth, comes, He will guide you into all the truth; for He will not speak on His own initiative, but whatever He hears, He will speak; and He will disclose to you what is to come.*

SOME PARTING THOUGHTS

As I look back on my journey towards heaven, since the day I surrendered my life to Jesus Christ – all I can say is I wish I hadn't waited so long to finally give myself to God. Really! Like so many people who don't know Jesus Christ as their Savior and Lord – I had to find out for myself just how lost and broken I was before I was ready to turn my life over to God.

The truth is the "fun and thrill" of being in the world chasing an elusive dream of being a "rock star" - or simply getting stoned and partying to the wee morning hours – had lost it's attraction. B.B.King[10], the late great Blues singer/guitarist had a lyric that says it all: "The thrill is gone baby!" Man O Man – that was certainly true for me and I was looking for something that would satisfy and fill the emptiness and longing deep in my heart.

That "something" turned out to be be "someone." Jesus Christ

It's funny how we like to say, I found God, or I found Jesus; when in reality He found us. He is always looking for us – for lost sheep – lost souls; that is what Jesus does. He chases us to the ends of the earth to rescue us from sin, this fallen and corrupt world, and of course – ourselves. I like to say God finds those who are looking for Him; but in reality His love is so incredible that God goes after those who never give a thought about Him – about God. That kind of love is beyond my comprehension – but that is why God is God.

It's hard to give control of our lives to anyone – that's just human nature. In my case, I learned very quickly from living on the streets and being immersed in a world of drugs, illicit sex, and lawlessness; that this world is a very scary and evil place for anyone – especially when God is not included. That was me. But as the old adage goes: "Better late than never." was certainly true with me... I like to say "God likes leftovers!"

He must because so many of us lost sheep only allow God into our lives after we have spent much of our lives chasing our own fleshly desires, only to discover later after making a mess of things – it was all a waste of time. The good news is God not only forgives our wretched past – with all of it's sinful consequences; but gives us a new heart and a clean conscience! Now that is something to get excited about.

It's amazing that some of us have to be dragged to the cross of Jesus as a last resort, and only after we have exhausted every possible excuse and bad choice in our search for happiness. I love the stubborn and unrelenting love of Jesus – who never stops pursuing us until we either surrender to His Lordship; or sadly reject Him and go our own way into darkness.

When you look at it that way – it seems like such an easy choice; but as the Bible reveals it's not – people are just not eager or ready to give their lives to God even if that means making a train wreck of our lives in the process!

Thankfully, God is always there – and His tender mercies are new every morning. God was always bring people and circumstances into my life, that were "signs" along the way pointing me to Jesus Christ. I'm grateful for all the godly people who God arranged for me to cross paths with while I was stumbling along my merry way to hell. I firmly believe that God gives all of us opportunities to choose between good and evil, between doing whats right or doing what's wrong... Free will comes with a price!

I'm so glad that I let Jesus find me – and save me. I know the best is yet to come, when I finally see Him face to face. Knowing this earth is not our final destination is very comforting, especially as we see so much hate, crime, and violence all around us. As things get worse and worse , it's good to know God is still in control and He has a wonderful plan for each person He has created.

As a Christian, the hope of heaven and being with Jesus and all the saints, and being reunited with friends and family that have gone on before us is powerful motivation to keep keeping on! This is not our home – so I have remind myself that I have to keep my eyes on Jesus and press on regardless of how dark or oppressive the world around us may be...

We are just here for a brief time, and then we can finally go to our permanent home in heaven. That is something I really look forward to.

If you are a Christian now, and have already given your life to Jesus Christ, I pray this book has added to your spiritual life in some positive way If you have not surrendered your life to Christ I encourage you to not wait a minute longer – you can pray right now for Jesus to come into your life and to give you a new heart. Just pray the simple prayer below.

Father God, I thank you for sending your son Jesus to die for my sins. Jesus I give you my life – all of it. I ask You to forgive me for all my sins, and cleanse me with your blood that you gave for all of us on the cross. Thank You for dying for me – for everyone. I believe you died on the cross for me and rose from the dead triumphant over death and Satan. In Your name Jesus I pray this prayer. Amen.

If you prayed this simple prayer - asking Jesus to save you from your sins, please write us at: litd.min@gmail.com Also, we invite you to visit our ministry website at: lightinthedarkministries.com There you will find out more about our worldwide ministry and other things to help you grow in your walk with God. We want to hear from you and please let us know if this book was a blessing to you or someone you may have shared it with.

Finally, let me ask you to pray for our ministry/Light in the Dark Ministries, and also ask you to visit some of our other online sites. Below are some places you can find some of my music and videos. If you want to help support our ministry financially – you can donate online at our website.

LIGHT IN THE DARK MINISTRIES

http://www.lightinthedarkministries.com

https://www.n1m.com/fool4christ

https://www.reverbnation.com/fool4christ

https://fool4christ.com

https://www.facebook.com/godsongs

https://twitter.com/fool4christusa

https://www.linkedin.com/in/fool4christ

fool4christusa@gmail.com

* You may find Michael's first book: Pearls of Wisdom / a collection of short stories/poems & other amusing writings from a Christian perspective that may surprise you... available on Amazon in print or Kindle.

ABOUT THE AUTHOR

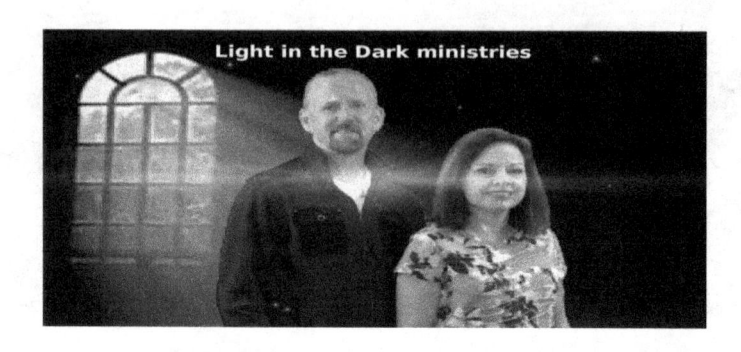

Michael D'Aigle is a Christian author and singer/songwriter who lives with his wife Deborah in Michigan. They have two sons, and are involved in have been actively involved in multi-faceted Christian ministries for many years. Michael is currently the U.S. Manager for Language Development System L.D.S., which teaches English to Koreans in South Korea. http://wetutorenglish.net

For the last few years before the Covid-19 pandemic hit America and the rest of the world; Michael and his wife were involved with ministry and outreach to the homeless, prisoners in jail and prison, and other evangelistic work mostly here in Michigan.

In 2009, they founded Light in the Dark Ministries, which is a worldwide ministry that partners with other Christian organizations and ministries from nations all over the earth. The emphasis is on providing prayer, guidance, and support in many different ways to those who are "friends & partners" with them. We have been able to build websites for free form many of those who needed that kind of help. The fellowship that results from these relationships has enriched all of those involved. http://www.lightinthedarkministries.com

Michael & Deborah own GODSONGS Music Production, a Christian recording studio that is devoted to producing Christian music exclusively; and works with Christian singers/bands/songwriters from all over the world.

This studio is able to do audio/video production from start to finish in an atmosphere that inspires great creativity for the kingdom of God.

You can visit their video websites at: http://www.godsongsusa.com https://www.facebook.com/godsongsusa and write them at: godsongs4u@gmail.com

Michael/fool4christ has released 9 musical albums to date with over 12,000,000 people who have visited his music sites around the world. He has published one book: Pearls of Wisdom that is available now in both print and digital format for Kindle readers on Amazon. He is currently finishing his 10th collection of songs that will be released under the title: Run To The Light – which should be out by the end of 2020. All of Michael's music can be purchased at most online digital stores.

Michael has been involved with leading praise & worship for many decades, either as the worship leader or simply helping out on bass or guitar/vocals as part of the praise team. At this time, Michael's main focus is on writing articles/blogs or working on new songs which is just an ongoing process for someone who never can say - "that was the last song I'll write."

"As long as God keeps giving me new songs, I'll just keep on recording them." "With God there is never an end to new ideas for songs – there is just no end to the immeasurable gifts that God gives us."

You can write Michael & his wife Deborah via email at: litd.min@gmail.com

Or if you like you can write Michael if it's about his music or songs at: fool4christusa@gmail.com They would love to hear from you and please let them know how this book or their ministry has been a blessing to you.

You can donate to their ministry if you would like to by simply going to their ministry website at: http://www.lightinthedarkministries.com

Please pray for Michael & Deborah as they continue to take the gospel to the ends of the earth through the power of the internet. Your prayers and support are coveted and will allow them to grow and reach more and more people before Jesus Christ returns to gather His children home.

If you would like to know more about how to become a "partner and friend" of Light in the Dark Ministries; just send us the following info:

- 1. Your name and your personal testimony of how you came to faith in Jesus Christian's

- 2. Your Ministry name – or the name of your church or organization.

- 3. Pictures of you and your wife/family & pictures of your ministry activities.

- 4. What your vision and mission statement is if you have one.

- 5. What your Doctrinal statement of faith is.

We look forward to hearing from you about your Christian ministry, and hope we can together become partners and friends in reaching the world for Jesus Christ.

In Jesus Name / Michael & Deborah D'Aigle

THE APOSTLE'S CREED[11]

I believe in God, the Father Almighty,
maker of heaven and earth;

And in Jesus Christ his only Son, our Lord;
who was conceived by the Holy Spirit,
born of the Virgin Mary,
suffered under Pontius Pilate,
was crucified, dead, and buried;*
the third day he rose from the dead;
he ascended into heaven,
and sitteth at the right hand of God the Father Almighty;
from thence he shall come to judge the quick and the dead.

I believe in the Holy Spirit,
the holy catholic church,
the communion of saints,
the forgiveness of sins,
the resurrection of the body,
and the life everlasting. Amen.

THE NICENE CREED[12]

I believe in one God,
the Father almighty,
maker of heaven and earth,
of all things visible and invisible.

I believe in one Lord Jesus Christ,
the Only Begotten Son of God,
born of the Father before all ages.
God from God, Light from Light,

true God from true God,
begotten, not made, consubstantial with the Father;
through him all things were made.
For us men and for our salvation
he came down from heaven,

and by the Holy Spirit was incarnate of the Virgin Mary,
and became man.

For our sake he was crucified under Pontius Pilate,
he suffered death and was buried,
and rose again on the third day
in accordance with the Scriptures.
He ascended into heaven
and is seated at the right hand of the Father.
He will come again in glory
to judge the living and the dead
and his kingdom will have no end.

I believe in the Holy Spirit, the Lord, the giver of life,
who proceeds from the Father and the Son,
who with the Father and the Son is adored and glorified,
who has spoken through the prophets.

I believe in one, holy, catholic and apostolic Church.
I confess one Baptism for the forgiveness of sins
and I look forward to the resurrection of the dead
and the life of the world to come

Out of the Darkness

HERE ARE MY MUSICAL RECORDINGS STARTING WITH MY EARLIEST RELEASES UP TO THE PRESENT.

Michael D'Aigle / fool4christ

1. THE LAST DAYS

https://music.apple.com/us/album/the-last-days/1271677452

2. HE'S COMING BACK

https://music.apple.com/us/album/hes-coming-back/1274532299

3. THIS IS WAR

https://music.apple.com/us/album/this-is-war/1269057854

4. 1ST DAY IN HEAVEN

https://music.apple.com/us/album/1st-day-in-heaven/1391889686

5. DANCE IN YOUR LIGHT

https://music.apple.com/us/album/dance-in-your-light/1258593977

6. AN INVISIBLE WORLD

https://music.apple.com/us/album/an-invisible-world/1266283426

7. BEAUTIFUL DUST

https://music.apple.com/us/album/beautiful-dust/1259830499

8. THE DAY OF THE LORD

https://music.apple.com/us/album/the-day-of-the-lord/1391807382

9. FOOL FOR CHRIST

https://music.apple.com/us/album/fool-for-christ/1475079541

10. DANCING WITH THE DEVIL (not published)

END NOTES

1. **Jimi Hendrix** (born **Johnny Allen Hendrix;** November 1951 27, 1942 – September 18, 1970) was an American rock guitarist, singer, and songwriter.

2. **Richard Allen "Dick" Wagner** (December 14, 1942 – July 30, 2014) was an American rock music guitarist, songwriter and author best known for his work with Alice Cooper, Lou Reed, and Kiss. He also fronted his own Michigan-based bands, the Frost and the Bossmen.

3. The **Hells Angels Motorcycle Club (HAMC)** is a worldwide one-percenter motorcycle club whose members typically ride Harley-Davidson motorcycles. The organization is "predominantly white male"[5]and is considered an organized crime syndicate by the United States Department of Justice.

4. Dianetics: The Modern Science of Mental Health (sometimes abbreviated as (**DMSMH)** is a book by L. Ron Hubbard about Dianetics, a system of psychotherapy he developed from a combination of personal experience, basic principles of Eastern philosophy, and the work of psychoanalysts such as Freud.

5. **Lafayette Ronald Hubbard** (March 13, 1911 – January 24, 1986), better known as **L. Ron Hubbard** (/εl rɒn-ˈhʌˌbərd/ɛʟʟ-ron-ʜᴜʙ-ərd[2]) and often referred to by his initials,**LRH,** was an American author and the founder of the Church of Scientology.

6. **"Only the Strong Survive"** is a song written by Jerry Butler,Kenny GambleandLeon Huff and originally sung in 1968 by Jerry Butler, released on his album *The Ice Man Cometh*. It was the most successful single of his career, reaching #4 on the *Billboard* Hot 100and was #1 for two weeks on the *Billboard* Black Singles Chart, in March and April 1969, respectively.[1]

7. Jerry LeBloch was the drummer for Rare Earth (1985–1990), an American Rhythm and blues/blues rock band. He took over for Bobby Rock (1985) and was later replaced by Dean Boucher (1990–1993).

8. **Free love** is a social movement that accepts all forms of love. The Free Love movement's initial goal was to separate the state from sexual matters such as marriage, birth control, and adultery. It claimed that such issues were the concern of the people involved, and no one else.

9. *Jesus freak* is a term arising from the late 1960s and early 1970s counterculture and is frequently used as a pejorative for those involved in the Jesus movement. As Tom Wolfe illustrates in *The Electric Kool-Aid Acid Test*, the term "freak" with a preceding qualifier was a strictly neutral term and described any counterculture member with a specific interest in a given subject; hence "acid freak" and "Jesus freak."

10. B.B.King **Riley B. King** (September 16, 1925 – May 14, 2015), known professionally as **B.B. King**, was an American singer-songwriter, guitarist, and record producer. King introduced a sophisticated style of soloing based on fluid string bending and shimmering vibrato that influenced many later blues electric guitar players. See: http://www.bbking.com/

11. **The Apostle's Creed** The Apostles' Creed is trinitarian in structure with sections affirming belief in God the Father, God the Son, and God the Holy Spirit.[2] The Apostles' Creed was based on Christian theological understanding of the canonical gospels, the letters of the New Testament and to a lesser extent the Old Testament. Its basis appears to be the old Roman Creed known also as the Old Roman Symbol.

12. **The Nicene Creed** is a statement of belief widely used in Christian liturgy. It is called *Nicene* /ˈnaɪsiːn/ because it was originally adopted in the city of Nicaea (present day İznik, Turkey) by the First Council of Nicaea in 325.[1] In 381, it was amended at the First Council of Constantinople, and the amended form is referred to as the Nicene or the Niceno-Constantinopolitan Creed. It defines Nicene Christianity.

Ten Books Every Believer Should Read

1. *Mere Christianity,* by C. S. Lewis

2. *The Harbinger,* by Jonathan Cahn

3. *The Cost of Discipleship,* by Dietrich Bonhoeffer

4. *The Pilgrim's Progress,* by John Bunyan

5. *The Imitation of Christ,* by Thomas a Kempis

6. *Knowing God,* by J. I. Packer

7. *The Hiding Place,* by Corrie ten Boom

8. *My Utmost For His Highest,* by Oswald Chambers

9. *The Spiritual Man,* by Watchman Nee

10. *Foxe's Book Of Martyrs,* by John Foxe

SOURCE MATERIALS

1. https://en.wikipedia.org/wiki/Wikipedia:About

2. https://www.biblegateway.com

3. The New King James Version Bible

CPSIA information can be obtained
at www.ICGtesting.com
Printed in the USA
BVHW050205060323
659724BV00025B/591